Papa was a Fisherman

by JOE B. LONG

[signature: Joe Long]

BARRE PUBLISHERS
Barre, Massachusetts
1969

Copyright © 1969 by Barre Publishing Co., Inc.
Library of Congress Catalog Card No. 69-19638
Standard Book Number 8271-6910-8
All rights reserved

Contents

1	The Little Mouse and the Big Bass	1
2	Pioneer Flyfisherman of the Great Smokies	8
3	Sevierville and Cades Cove	21
4	The Women	28
5	The Charmed Life	33
6	"On Top of Old Smoky"	43
7	Life on the Ohio	49
8	Home Was a Place of Laughter	59
9	Pace Whitestone	68
10	The Nativity on Tour	77
11	Special Delivery	86
12	"Fly Fishing is a Gentleman's Sport"	90

To The Grandchildren
of The Fisherman

Joe, Joan, Angela
Patty, Clifton

Foreword

At the turn of the century an alert, muscular man found his way into the wilderness of what is now The Great Smoky Mountains National Park. He had journeyed from his boyhood home on the Ohio River. In his pack he carried oil paints, a roll of canvas and camel hair brushes. His slouch hat was decorated with a vari-color of hand-tied flies and protruding from the pack were the slender disjointed pieces of a light fly rod.

From lonesome "hollers" and cabins, perched high on creek banks, men who had been summoned by the mysterious "Mountain Telegraph" came to spy him out. It was the day of the clandestine "still" and the corn liquor mash boiled and bubbled in copper pots by small running waters, the wispy smoke of secret fires mixing with the haze of the mountains. The mountain men came with stealth to watch the intruder for "Revenuooers" often disguised themselves as fishermen.

This man was somehow different and they couldn't quite make him out. He didn't have the look of the law and they were at a total loss to understand why he had "them bugs" stuck in the band of his hat.

They watched him take the strange fish pole from his pack and put it together. He plucked a "bug" from his hat and tied it to the end of his line. He cast upon the water and fish rose and struck it. They saw him bring forth great strings of black bass and rainbow trout and to them it was magic for they had never imagined such a thing.

The stranger became a part of the wilderness and the mountaineer accepted him. He spent nights in their cabins and ate of their simple fare with relish. They watched him sit in the shade of a tulip poplar with the north light falling across his canvas. They marveled to see him capture the far-off vistas of the mountains, even to the violet mist with which they were enshrouded.

He taught them to tie flies with the feathers from their roosters and bucktails from the hair of a hound-dog or a raccoon. Among the mountain men there were true fishermen and they became his converts.

In many ways the man was like the mountaineer. He was at home in the wilderness and its solitude and danger held no fear. He had the mountain man's fierce spirit of independence, his need to be free, a yearning for the balm found in rushing stream and virgin forest. He was rather a remarkable man who was able to fill his life with exciting adventure. He did a variety of things well but I think he was at his very best standing in a rushing stream casting the lure. For this reason when I am asked about my father I say, "First of all Papa was a fisherman."

CHAPTER I

The Little Mouse and the Big Bass

"Painter" creek rushed out of the foothills of the Great Smokies and joined the Little Tennessee as it leveled into the plain of the Tennessee Valley.

Fifty years ago a log cabin was perched on the high bank overlooking the clear pool where the streams had their confluence. I hope it still stands but I shall not risk returning to see, for I have found that the fondly remembered scenes of youth are best not revisited. Papa and I had been fishing up Panther Creek. We had intended to tramp across the mountain to catch the train for Knoxville but Papa had fished until dark and by that time it was too late to return home.

You could always count on mountain hospitality and when we climbed the narrow path to the cabin we were greeted by the baying of the hounds with which all such dwellings were populated. I was twelve years old and very embarrassed about begging food and shelter. The mountaineer came to the door with a kerosene lamp in his hand and we were welcomed in to stand by a big log fire.

We were dripping wet and shivering from the penetrating chill. Papa never wore waders. He was dressed in one of his good suits, a pair of hobnail boots and a collar and tie.

The owner of the cabin proved to be a preacher. "You are welcome to spend the night and to partake of what we have," he said with dignity, "but you are cold and wet. I am not a drinking man myself but I believe a glass of spirits would keep you from catching cold," and with that he brought forth a stone jug with a corncob stuck in the end of it. He poured out the clear liquid in a heavy glass tumbler, Papa protesting at the quantity.

"I'd like a little hot water in it and some sugar," Papa said.

They had no sugar but they had honey, "sweetnin" they called it. Sugar was rare in the mountains but honey was a fine substitute. The mountaineer used it for many purposes. He even poured it into the radiator of his "T-Model" for "anti-freeze." No mountain cabin was complete without bee hives, and bee trees were often robbed for wild honey.

After the toddy was prepared Papa invited our host to have a drink with him. Again protesting that he was not a drinking man, the preacher proceeded to pour a full tumbler of "White Mule" for himself. The glass never left his lips until he had drained the last drop. Later Papa told me, "If I hadn't seen it, I never would have believed that a man could do it. Why, that glass held a good half pint!"

We had a supper of "Hogback" and turnip greens topped off with "Berry Leather". At the time of the fruit harvest the mountain woman placed long thin rolls of dough on the cabin roof in the sun. Into the roll she pressed apples, peaches, berries. When they were completely dehydrated she moistened the concoction sufficiently so that it could be fashioned into a long, thick roll which was hung outside in the cabin eaves. Dropped into boiling water it quickly came to life and made a delicious pudding.

The preacher and his wife went off to bed. She had said scarcely a word since our arrival. The mountain woman had the sterling virtue of speaking only when spoken to!

Papa and I undressed in front of the fire and hung our wet clothes up to dry. We occupied the tiny bedroom which belonged to the daughters who were visiting "kinfolk t'other side of the mountain." On the back of the bedroom door hung two old-fashioned nightgowns. Despite my protests Papa put one of them on and ordered me to do likewise. I can see him now - his muscular, hairy frame enveloped in the folds of the nightdress with the huge puffed sleeves billowing up to his ears. I was so completely enveloped that I couldn't walk to the bed without holding up my skirts.

We climbed into the high four-poster and lay down on the shuck mattress. Every time one of us moved, it sounded like the roof was falling in but we were warm and comfortable and were soon dead to the world.

It seemed I had barely fallen asleep when Papa wakened me. "Time to get up," he said and I could hear the preacher and his wife moving about in the next room. It was pitch dark outside.

The cabin was situated between two mountains so that the sun did not reach it until ten o'clock and it "set" about two in the afternoon.

Papa sat on the edge of the bed and began putting on his

boots. Papa's fishing boots were unique. He got tired of struggling with wet rawhide laces and he had a shoemaker rivet in a series of buttons on one side and matching hooks on the other. It took but a few minutes to button up his boots with the aid of a button-hook which was a part of his equipment. As he ran his foot into the first boot he began dancing around the floor trying to kick it off.

"There's something in my boot," he yelled.

After he got it off he ran his hand inside and came out with a tiny woods mouse which had crawled in during the night.

Papa smoked a small cigar called "Virginia Cheroots". He had designed the box for the manufacturer, a friend of his. He painted a brood sow lying on her side with fourteen teats exposed. Ten little pigs were nursing and the caption read, "She Roots, Fourteen for Ten." Holding the little mouse, he had me remove the cigars and punch holes in the box with my knife. Then he put the mouse inside and stuck the box in the pocket of his coat. I kept after him all day, trying to find out what he planned to do with the mouse but he wouldn't tell me.

We fished down the Little Tennessee, or rather Papa did for I soon tired and dawdled along the bank or sat in the shade watching him catch fish.

About noon we discovered a crossroads store. Papa bought a bag of the best groceries afforded for he knew the mountaineer would refuse to take money for our lodgings.

We arrived back at the cabin late in the afternoon. The preacher's wife cooked our fish and we ate fish and corn pone until we couldn't hold any more.

THE LITTLE MOUSE AND THE BIG BASS

After supper Papa said, "Come along, Joe, and I'll show you how to catch the biggest bass in Panther Creek."

At this hour the water in the big pool was black as night. Deep in shadow and across from where we stood was a huge rock about the size of the cabin. "There is a big bass who lives right in the eddy of that rock," Papa said. "He's run everything else out of the pool and he's just waiting for this little mouse."

"What if he isn't hungry?"

"The bass is a fighter. He'll be either hungry or mad, probably both," Papa said.

On the bank was a woodlot and the ground was covered with chips. Papa selected one the size of his hand. He took the mouse out of the box, pulled back the skin at the scruff of its neck and ran the hook of the "Parmachina Bell" through the skin. He crept to the upper edge of the pool, put the mouse on the chip and the current began to carry the little fellow slowly toward the big rock as Papa played out the line. The mouse clung desperately to the chip and just as it swung toward the backwater Papa jerked him off and the tiny animal began a desperate swim for the shore.

Suddenly the surface of the water boiled up. The bass had struck and the battle was on!

The Shakespeare fly rod weighed four ounces and the bass was a monster. What's more, he was none of your potbellied lake bass but a cold water specimen, built like a torpedo and possessed with a savage cunning. He began by leaping high into the air, shaking his head in a desperate attempt to dislodge the hook. The rod bent almost double and Papa scrambled up and down to keep his line from fouling in the low hanging trees and bushes. These maneuvers took him in and out of the stream. The pool was deep and often he was in up to his armpits holding the rod high above his head, never allowing the line to slacken.

When the bass failed to shake the hook, he headed for the river. Papa fought hard to keep him in the pool. Fortunately there was room to play the fish. The pool was at least forty yards long. The light test line was a problem and Papa had to take care not to put too much strain on it. He would work the bass up to the head of the pool and then let him run toward the river. The battle was complicated by a sunken log above the rock and the bass made repeated attempts to get under it. "I can't let him get to that log or he'll foul the line," Papa yelled.

I was running up and down the bank, shouting and getting in the way. My cries brought the preacher and he was as excited as I was. "I been tryin' to catch that fish ever since I moved here three years ago," he yelled. "My God, I'm afeared you'll never git him in with that willow stick of yourn." But by this time, and almost a half hour had gone by, the fish was beginning to tire. Papa steered him toward a little sandy bar and the old monarch lay there looking up at us with a baleful eye from the shallow clear water. Papa put his hand under his prize and lifted him bodily out of the water and laid him on the sand. The old fellow was too spent to move. The three of us stood there admiring his beauty and great size.

"Never seed anything like it," the preacher said. "I knowed he was a big un but not that big."

Papa got out his pocket scales. The bass pulled four pounds four ounces. With a pair of pliers Papa cut the hook in half and worked the smooth end out of the mouth.

There were two other hooks there, both old and rusty, and he removed them. One had about two feet of line trailing from it.

Then Papa put the old fighter back into the pool. The fish lay there balancing himself with the pectoral fins and then with a leisurely flick of his huge tail he disappeared into the black depths and his lair behind the stone.

"Mister," the preacher said, "I'm right glad you done that. I'd feel mighty lonesome without that thar fish — yes sir, I would. That was a true act of kindness. I honor a man who loves God's critters and you're right welcome to stay with us anytime you're in these parts."

CHAPTER 2

Pioneer Fly Fisherman of the Great Smokies

Our family moved to East Tennessee in 1906. The Appalachian Mountains were then a vast wilderness. There were few roads and only the trails blazed by three generations of pure Scotch-Irish mountain folk made them at all accessible. There were logging operations in a few places and one could hitch a ride on the narrow gauge railway which had its base in Townsend. This petered out in a few miles and you were on your own.

Papa loved the wilderness and he was as much at home in it as the mountaineer. It was a land of many wonders. Due to the heavy rainfall and temperate climate it contained more and varied types of plant life than any other place in the world ... giant tulip poplars, pine, hemlock and entire forests of chestnuts. Most of it was virgin, never invaded by the axeman.

Fruits were abundant. There were muscadines and fields of wild berries. I can remember coming across a crystal pool and picking ice cold blackberries, their canes having been pulled into the clear mountain water by the sheer weight of abundance. There was Papaw, a sweet banana-like delicacy belonging to the *Asimina triloba* or custard-apple family with their beautiful purple blooms. Occasionally one came across a burned-out cabin, its stone chimney still standing, and beside it a tree bending with yellow summer apples.

In no other region were the wild flowers in such profligate abundance. In the springtime entire mountainsides would be in bloom with azalea; "Flame Azalea" it is called for at a distance the mountains appear to be on fire. There were the rhododendron and laurel, trout lilies and trillium to mention but a few of the more spectacular. There was a nodding trillium or wake-robin, the painted trillium and the purple variety that has the unpleasant odor of decayed flesh and is propagated not by the bee but by the gadfly. There were veritable carpets of hepatica, lady slipper, showy orchids, and on and on ad infinitum.

The forest abounded with animal life . . . black bear, bobcat, foxes, deer and wolves. There were raccoons, opossum and a variety of fur bearers of the genus *Mustela*. One evening at dusk I came face to face with a magnificent albino fox. We stood staring at each other and after a time he trotted leisurely off down the trail.

Papa brought home chameleons, little lizards which change color to camouflage themselves in harmony with their environment. One day we caught a tiny red squirrel, "mountain boomers" they were called. These nocturnal animals sail from tree to tree by means of a membrane which stretches between the front and hind legs. He was very tame and would crawl into my pocket and go to sleep. One night as we were sitting by the campfire he crawled out and flew into the flames.

The birds were without number, birds of song and birds of prey. Huge owls, hawks and majestic eagles which kept the life of forest and stream in balance. Snakes abounded, both harmless and deadly. There were black racers, pine snakes, hognose and the banded water snake. The latter were called "water moccasins" by the mountaineer but were not the deadly cottonmouth found in the swamps further south. These snakes would sun themselves on rocks in the streams and it was great sport to gig them with the fly. In the water they would give you a great fight but you had to risk being bitten in disengaging the hook. The bite was about like a bee sting. The diamond back rattlesnake was the scourge of the mountains. Often in country stores huge rattlers would be on display in wire cages. For the most part they had been chloroformed and the poison sack removed.

The copperhead issued his warning by the pungent odor of fresh cucumbers and of course the whirring sound of the rattler was unmistakable. He didn't always have time to sound his warning and many people were bitten stepping across a log.

The story is told of the Italian laborer working on the railroad who was warned to listen for the rattle. One day he stepped right into a den and was struck a sharp blow on the boot. He jumped back in a state of panic managing to yell, "You Son-of-a-Gunna, why you no ringga-dat bell!"

The rattler liked to bask in warm places and under the heat of the sun became very sluggish. I killed one with a fence rail as he lay on the railroad track. He was seven feet long. I knew a mountain woman who found a rattlesnake curled up on the bed beside her sleeping baby!

The people of the mountains were the most interesting of all. The only remaining pure stock on this continent, they were a proud and independent race. Illiterate but not ignorant; superstitious but hospitable, they clung to the legends, superstitions, speech and religious beliefs of their Scotch-Irish ancestors. They were fiercely patriotic, and in the midst of secession the mountain men fought with the Union in the War Between the States.

The mountaineer had a problem with the law. He believed as long as he raised his corn that he was entitled to do with it as he well pleased, and clandestine stills sprang up along the creeks and rivulets. This began a war, often to the death with the "Revenooers." To make liquor running water is required and a fire to boil the "mash." Fire meant smoke, only a small wisp if care was used, but smoke nevertheless and this made the still vulnerable to detection. The "mountain telegraph" was born and proved to be even more effective than the jungle drums although it was never discovered exactly how it worked. A stranger could not set foot into this domain without the awareness of the dwellers for miles around.

One summer morning Papa, my brother Frank and I left the narrow-gauge railroad and hiked across the mountain carrying a letter from a friend to one Harrison Moore, whom we had never seen. On the trail we met a man with a woman and a "passel" of children. He was carrying a rifle and his woman was in her place, a good ten yards behind.

"I'm looking for Harrison Moore," Papa said.

"Well he ain't home — passed his place this mornin', and he ain't home."

"I've got a letter from Jim Birdsong telling him that we're up here to fish."

The mountaineer took the letter and turned it over and over and said nothing.

"Tell me what Mr. Moore looks like so I'll know him when I see him," Papa said.

There was a long pause during which the man continued to look us over.

"Well, I'm him," he said at last.

My mother was not much for camping but Papa discovered an abandoned storehouse in Cades Cove and the four of us left Sevierville one morning and headed for the Cove in a spring wagon drawn by two mountain mules. We had no more than established ourselves with our "plunder" (as the mountain folk referred to all possessions) before we had visitors. They had tramped over the trails to get a look at the strangers. Men, women and children sat off at a distance and watched us eat our supper in front of the cabin, following each bite from hand to mouth. Many of them had never seen "light bread," none had tasted peanut butter, and bananas were unknown.

The story is told of the mountaineer who refused to eat a banana. "Don't think I better," he said. "I got so many tastes now I can't satisfy them all and I don't want no more."

Mama put peanut butter on a piece of bread and handed it to a young woman. The girl rolled it over her tongue, made a wry face and spit it out.

"Are you married?" Mama asked her.

"No Mam, I haint," the girl answered.

About that time a small boy ran to her calling "Ma."

"Is that your baby," Mama asked.

"Well-yesum hit is."

"I thought you said you weren't married."

"Well, I haint, but I was feelin' poorly and the Doc told

me if I'd fotch a kid I'd git better. Well, I fotched one and sure 'nuf I did!"

Mama was fascinated by the picturesque speech of the mountain people. Mountain women loved flowers and around their cabins was a bright array of bloom grown in broken pottery and tin cans. They called their dahlia bulbs "Dally Taters." ("I've never been refused hospitality where there were flowers," Papa once told me.)

Near one of the cabins was a spring which boiled up at intervals. One of the women told my Mother that "Hit is a fitified spring."

Mama visited one of the cabins wearing a trim cotton dress. The mountain woman who would have made three of my dainty Mother challenged her with "Miz Long, I'll throw you down for that dress."

As she sat with one of the children on her knee the mountain man spoke up—"Miz Long, when we heard you was a-comin' we was skeered that a fine-haired woman like you would look-down on us poor folks,—but Miz Long, I do declare that you air one of the commonest women we has ever seed!"

Of Papa's many friends among the mountain people one of them stands out in my memory. He was many men rolled into one - guide, carpenter, stone mason and the father of fourteen children. At one time he owned a small furniture shop in Gatlinburg, graced by a crude sign which read — "Genuine Antiques made to order."

Papa made a date with him to meet us at the railroad and take us into the "blowdown," a tangled wilderness into which it was dangerous to venture without a guide. We waited for two hours but Wiley failed to show up.

Papa saw him later and asked why he hadn't kept the appointment.

"Well, Mr. Long," he said, "hit was the old womern—she was mighty bad."

"What was the trouble," Papa asked.

"She had one of them misgoes," was the reply.

It was about this time that Henry Ford visited the mountains seeking early Americana for his Dearborn Museum. Wiley had many things which the great industrialist wanted to buy. One was a huge flour sifter. The frame made of a piece of hickory which had been steamed and bent into a circle. Between were woven black and white tail hairs of horses in an intricate design. It was a thing of rare beauty, in daily use, and Wiley saw no reason to part with it.

However he and Mr. Ford "hit-it-off" real well and he vowed that he would name his next child, already on the way, after the great man. The baby turned out to be a girl, but true to his word it was christened "Mrs. Henry Ford Stokley."

Mrs. Ford, hearing of the honor, sent the child a beautiful handmade dress. When the mother received it she ripped out the hand stitches and took it down the mountain to a woman who owned a sewing machine. "Does look like a womern with as much money as Miz Ford would git herself a sewin' machine," she remarked.

The mountaineer was a man of fierce loyalties and especially to his kin. A wrong done to a relative, however distant, was counted a personal wrong to be avenged, and feuds sprang up in which killing for killing resulted. These were encouraged by the habit of getting "liquored up" on moonshine.

After our meeting on the trail with Harrison Moore and his family, we became great friends and were always welcome into his domain. Moore was a "moonshiner" and hid his liquor in the bushes about a hundred yards from the cabin. If you wandered out back one of the boys would chase after you and call out, "Don't go out thar, them bees will sting you."

Revenue agents were killed and mountain men were sometimes caught and brought to justice. I remember seeing a huge copper still displayed in the courthouse yard at Sevierville and I also recall seeing two men hanging from a scaffold in that same place. Wes Wynn was the Federal Marshal of Sevier County. It was said that he could drop a match box, draw and drill it before it hit the ground although I never saw him do it.

The corn liquor they made was pretty mean stuff. It was often drunk right after it was skimmed off and the result could be a complete change of personality. It was called Corn Squeezin, White Mule, White Lit'nin, Mountain Dew, Stonewall Jackson's Revenge, and so on. It was mostly drunk out of a jug and straight.

Judge Sanford was the Federal Judge in Knoxville during the mooshine era. He was afterward appointed to the United States Supreme Court and died in office. The Judge told Papa about a preacher whom he had sent to Atlanta for moonshining. The agents knew he made whisky but because he was a good influence in the community of Cosby, they let him alone. One dark night they caught him on the road with a full load in his truck and they had to take him in. The Judge sentenced him to a year and a day in the Atlanta Penitentiary. When he had served his time he stopped by to see the Judge on his way home. "Jedge, I want to thank you for sending me down to Atlanta," he said. "Why, I had never been out of my county before and I met a lot of interestin' people down to Atlanta. They had a fine library in the penitentiary and I got in a lot of good readin'. But Judge, I want to ask a favor of you. They tell me old Henry Sykes has stole some of my labels and is puttin' them on that rot gut liquor of his'n and I want you to send somebody up thar to stop him because efen you don't he is sure gonna ruin my business."

In the very early days fire was necessary to the survival of the mountaineer and it was at times not easily come by. Many old families had fires which were never allowed to go out. It was not uncommon for children to be sent to the nearest cabin to borrow fire which they carried home in an iron pot. When the National Park was established and the mountain families were moved out of their homes, the Yanceys loaded their fire in the big iron cooking pot and took it with them to their new location in the foothills.

Into this vast wilderness with its breathtaking beauty Papa entered with his flies and fly rod. Intruders were rare and the mountain folk for miles around soon knew of his presence. He was referred to as "that funny little man with them bugs in his hat."

The mountaineer caught trout and black bass. Indeed they were an important part of his limited diet. For the most part he caught fish not as a sportsman but as a "pot fisherman" and in various and sundry ways. The true fisherman . . . and you will find him wherever you go . . . used a long cane pole and for the trout he baited the larvae of the wasp. He would hop with amazing agility from rock to rock, fishing up stream and dropping his line into deep pools or white water depending upon the season.

PIONEER FLY FISHERMAN OF THE GREAT SMOKIES

For the "pot fisherman" seining was a favorite in the larger streams although it was against the law, the mountaineer had neither respect nor understanding for what was called "conservation." The small mouth bass soon learned to jump over the top of the seine. Papa was paddling across Little River in a dugout one dark night and I was in the bow holding a kerosene lantern. This apparently was a seining hole for the bass began leaping over the boat. One two-pounder failed to make the leap and landed squarely in my lap. In my excitement I dropped the lantern and grappled with the fish but he flopped out of my arms and back into the river.

"Fingering" was a favorite way to catch trout and was so productive that a law was passed prohibiting it. The fisherman would feel under a likely stone with his bare hand. If you were quiet and gentle the trout would allow you to stroke up and down his side without moving. The trout has no scales but a slippery slime all over his body and the only place you could hold him was at the gills. When you felt the gill openings you clamped down hard and came up with a fish. Trouble was that you couldn't always tell a trout from a water snake or the horrible ugly "Mud puppy."

There were a few dynamiters who would throw a stick into a pool, killing every creature within range of the explosion.

Papa was soon the friend and indeed the confidant of the mountain men for he had an irresistible personality and they recognized in him a kindred spirit. However, they continued to make fun of "them bugs" in his hat... that is, until they saw him catch fish. He came to their cabins with great strings which included many of the old "Residenters" which they had been unable to land. It was then that the real fishermen among the mountain men became his converts. He taught them how to tie flies. At that time no store in Knoxville stocked such a thing. Papa influenced the W. W. Woodruff Hardware Company in Knoxville to stock the first artificial lures ever sold in Eastern Tennessee.

How Papa could cast a fly! He could drop it behind a rock in a place you would have thought impossible. He could make it dart swiftly forward and suddenly break and change direction. He could flick it into a pool so that it struck the surface with hardly a ripple and then cause it to struggle feebly as the mayflies do when trying to free their wings for flight.

It was something to watch him fight a fish. He never used a landing net, and unless he could tire his catch so he could lift it out of the water with his hand, he did not consider it a fair contest. He released many of his fish but he furnished his friends, both in and out of the mountains, with his catch. There were no limits in the early days. Papa did not use a creel but put his fish on a stringer, dragging them through the water to keep them alive. Often the string was so heavy that he tied it out in a pool and went on fishing. At the end of the day it was my job to go back and retrieve them.

Late one afternoon Papa was fishing alone and had tied his catch far upstream. It was getting late and because it was rough country he leaned his rod against a tree and hiked back to pick up his fish. When he returned the rod was gone and he could see signs leading down the creek. Papa was an expert tracker and following through the undergrowth he found the man standing on a sandbar and casting clumsily into the stream with the missing fly rod.

Here was a delicate situation. The mountaineer was proud and easily offended. After all he hadn't stolen the rod, he had found it leaning against the tree. Papa spoke and stood watching.

"Nice looking rod you have there!" he remarked.

"Jist got it," was the reply. "Cost me five dollars."

"I'm a fly fisherman. Here, let me show you how to use it."

Papa took the rod out of the man's hand and began to cast. The mountaineer backed up against a tree and watched silently. He waded into the creek and continued his fly casting lesson. A short distance down the creek there was a bend in the stream, my father fished on. Just as he disappeared out of sight he threw up his hand in farewell. The mountaineer never moved.

Papa was not only a skillful fisherman but he was a persistent one. He offered the fly to a great many fish. Worn out I would follow him downstream until the light failed and I had to grope my way along. One day our friend, Jim Birdsong, went with us. It was dusk and we were sitting on the bank watching Papa fish. The bullbats were flying about overhead, feeding on the night bugs. I noticed one which kept making passes at his fly on the back cast. At last he caught it!

Papa thought he was hung up on a bush until he turned around and saw the hawk. The bird put up quite a fight. He carefully reeled him in, detached the hook and tossed him back into the air. By that time it was dark.

"Mr. Long," Jim Birdsong said, "you've caught all the fish in the river and now you're catching birds. It's about a mile down to the car. For heaven's sake let's go home!"

> (In a later chapter when I tell you about Papa's hunting exploits, I'll describe how he caught another bird in the air.)

Papa could catch fish where there were "no fish." I remember one time when there was a long dry spell and the stream was so low that the deep pools appeared to be stagnant. He had invited one of his friends, also a fly fisherman, to go along with us. Papa was a quarter of a mile ahead, down stream. We fished all day, off and on, without a single strike. In the later afternoon we caught up with Papa. He was sitting on a log smoking one of his cheroots.

"C. J., there just aren't any fish in this stream," our companion said. "A couple of hours ago I stopped fishing and began kicking under stones and I couldn't scare up a single fish."

"Oh, there are plenty of fish," Papa said.

"I don't believe it, let's see your fish."

Papa reached back into the bushes and pulled out a string of bass that knocked our eyes out. "To catch fish in this low water you have to keep the fly as far from you as possible. I've been casting to my very limit all day long."

In those distant days the land abounded with fish and game and Papa was in his heaven.. He left his stamp upon the wilderness and it upon him. He roamed its solitudes and wet his line in streams where few but he had ever fished. He drew from the mountains the inspiration expressed in beautiful landscapes and in their vastness he found the strengths by which he preserved his unique originality.

CHAPTER 3

Sevierville and Cades Cove

The activities of John Sevier run like a flaming thread through the early history of Tennessee. He fought in the battle of Kings Mountain leading an expedition across the Great Smoky Mountains to defeat the British. He fought the Cherokee Indians, organized the "Lost State of Franklin" and became its Governor, and when it was dissolved he joined the ranks of the outlaws. He was rescued by his friends who secured a pardon for him. When the State of Franklin became a part of the new State of Tennessee he was elected its first Governor and served for six terms. In the rolling foothills of the mountains which formed the backdrop for his many adventues stands the town which bears his name — Sevierville, Tennessee.

Sevierville was the base of many of our forays into the wilderness. I can remember journeying from Knoxville by stagecoach before the railroad was built. There were two coaches, passenger and mail. The passenger coach plugged along over the dusty roads with one team of horses but the mail changed horses three times between the two towns and made the trip at a bold gallop. Often I was allowed to sit on top with the driver. The vehicle swayed deliriously around the curves until one had to hang on to keep from falling from the high perch. Can you imagine a more thrilling experience for a small boy!

Uncle Jimmy Bowers ran the only hotel in Sevierville and our family often stayed there. Mama and my younger brother Frank would wait for Papa and me when we went into the mountains, and on rare occasions they went along, camping out in one of the coves which was accessible by mule team.

The fare at the Bowers Hotel was both generous and plain. Everything was covered by a thick brown crust, having been fried in deep hog fat. The string beans tasted much like the fried chicken.

I remember one Sunday when my mother could stand it no longer. With Uncle Jimmy's permission she invaded the kitchen, put on an apron and supervised the preparation of Sunday dinner. "I doubt if these people have ever tasted decent food," Mama said.

I remember we had stewed chicken, delicious light dumplings, fresh vegetables that tasted like vegetables and an unheard-of tomato salad. Uncle Jimmy and the guests tried to be complimentary but they ate the meal with something less than enthusiasm. It was plain to see that they were addicted to the greasy concoctions which formed their daily diet. I am told that those who have drunk cheap whisky for years find good Scotch and Bourbon unpalatable.

It was at the Bowers Hotel that Papa met a man who was to become one of his fast and enduring friends. He was a "drummer" for a wholesale grocery company in Knoxville and rode horseback through the mountains calling on isolated stores in the region.

Smith was not more than five feet five inches, ruddy of complexion and with one of the most winning personalities I have ever encountered. I do not know how he had developed it but his right arm was a third larger than his left and he could perform prodigious feats of strength which included chinning himself with that stout arm.

Twin tow-headed boys lived in the town and often played in front of the Hotel. Smith would grab one at a time by the hair, lift him clear off the ground and hold him at arm's length. Each boy weighed a good eighty pounds but Smith was able to perform this feat with no trouble at all. I was mighty jealous of these boys for when he tried to lift me by the hair I screamed with pain.

The Hotel had the usual porch which ran the length of the front of the building. One sunny afternoon the guests had adjourned there to sit supinely in rocking chairs so that their stomachs could struggle with that upon which they had gorged themselves. A team of work horses stood at the watering trough in the center of the square and Smith, who was playing with my baby brother, set him astride one of the horses. He was holding the baby in an upright position when a stray dog came yelping down the street. The horse took fright and bolted. Smith went down almost under the hoofs of the frightened horse. The side of his face was a bloody mess but that mighty right arm grasping my brother's dress held him aloft and free from harm. Frank gurgled delightedly, demanding "More, more!" Under Papa's tutelage Smith became an ardent fly fisherman. I hope it didn't cost him his job.

Cade's Cove, fifteen miles from Sevierville, was a favorite haunt. It was a small natural basin fastness surrounded by majestic peaks and watered by a crystal river and its tributaries which converged and lingered along the level ground. There we met "Black Bill" Walker, a dark and forbidding giant of a man who had five strapping daughters. Black Bill's cabin was surrounded by a stockade fence to keep the "varmints" out and every morning his daughters swept the front yard clean as a whistle. Not a blade of anything was allowed to grow in the yard.

Mama visited the Walkers. The mother had died years before and the girls kept house for Black Bill. They had no books except the old family Bible and they had never seen a magazine. Their reading material consisted of a dozen or so old farm implement catalogues which were dog-eared from use. When Papa and I went back into the Cove I carried a big bundle of *Saturday Evening Posts, Ladies Home Journals* and *The Country Gentleman.* When these magazines were opened it was a big day in the Cove!

And then there were the two Spinster Sisters, both in their nineties. They lived in a one-room cabin and did all their cooking in the big fireplace which extended almost the full length of one side of the room. The logs they burned were a good six feet long. When they needed wood they hitched an ancient white horse to a log. He pulled the log in through the front door; they unhitched at the fireplace and rolled the huge log onto the fire and then led the horse out through the back door, a real luxury in log cabins.

When I think of Cade's Cove I think of the spider and the butterflies. It is strange how amidst the unnumbered things which happen to us certain minor episodes remain in our memories. Perhaps the small things in our lives are more important than we ever know.

Papa and I were seated by the creek one sunny day. A string of fish was tied out in the bright pool and we were eating our lunch. I was dangling the fish in and out of the water when a pair of brilliant yellow swallowtails fluttered into view, changing hue as they gyrated aimlessly through sunlight and shadow. Suddenly one swooped down toward the water and was caught in the giant web of a spider which had fastened its lair to the rock on which I sat. The butterfly beats its wings in a panic of desperation, broke one golden pinion free, was entangled again and at last spent itself and lay quivering, suspended in the silken meshes of the web. As if answering the doorbell, the spider, whose body was the size of a man's thumb, emerged from its hole under the rock, surveyed his prey for a brief moment and began a slow advance. At sight of the spider the butterfly renewed its efforts to escape, and then - as if by magic - the air was suddenly filled with yellow butterflies. Some of them dove at the huge spider, fluttering above him, brushing him with their wings. Others hovered above as if to encourage the captive to break free. At last one member of the rescue corps was caught by the wing and in a brief time it too was hopelessly ensnared. The spider having been driven back into his den, reappeared and began another advance. Now Papa came at my call and we watched, fascinated by this battle for survival.

As the spider began his second sortie I slid from the rock onto the sandy beach, found a stick and advanced on the spider. "Let him alone, Joe," Papa called out.

"No, no, I must save the butterflies!" I cried and began beating at the spider who scuttled back to his hiding place.

I plunged the stick into the hole again and again. There was no sign of the spider. The strands of the web were torn away by my blows. The second butterfly, stronger because of the shortness of his captivity, released himself and flew off but the first victim dropped into the water and floated motionless into a shallow eddy. I waded into the stream, lifted him gently and placed him on a low hanging bush. Again the cloud of butterflies appeared out of nowhere and hovered over the victim.

"What are they doing, Papa?" I asked.

"I'm not sure," Papa said, "but it looks as if they are trying to dry him off with the air from their wings."

"Why didn't you want me to kill the spider, Papa?"

"The spider was full of eggs. She needed someplace to lay those eggs. If you had not interfered, she would have killed the butterfly with her poison bite. It wouldn't have hurt him, just put him to sleep. Then she would have dragged him into her den and laid her eggs inside his body. When the little spiders hatched they would have eaten the body of the butterfly until they were strong enough to catch food for themselves."

"I don't care. I'm glad I saved the butterfly and I hope I killed the spider. I don't like spiders. They are mean and ugly, but I love butterflies. They are beautiful."

"Their wings are beautiful but their bodies are no prettier than those of the spider."

"Don't you think spiders are ugly?" I pursued.

"No, not particularly," Papa said, "and your thinking them ugly would not make them so. You see, Son, beauty and ugliness exist only in our minds and our minds are very small. God made you and me and the butterflies and the spiders and in the sight of God none of his creatures is ugly and each is put on earth for a purpose. Each has a job to do and the job of the butterfly is to feed the spider. If there were no butterflies there would be no spiders, and if there were no spiders, there would be no butterflies. Each is a part of Nature's great plan. We cannot understand it but we know it is a perfect plan."

I remember the impression this made on me.

"Did I interfere with God's plan when I killed the spider?" I asked Papa.

"I don't think so, Joe," he said, "I imagine a small boy with a stick is a part of His plan, too!"

CHAPTER 4
The Women

After Sevierville

In our mountain wanderings Papa and I often came across tiny graveyards. They were pitiful places, so overgrown that you stumbled on them unawares. Manufactured headstones were few and the graves were marked by jagged pieces of slate slanted into the wind. These were scratched by barely legible names and dates. I remember one small plot where seven babies rested, all of the same mother and all dead in their first year.

"Where have all the Graveyards gone, long, long ago" sings the mountain ballad. Where indeed, for the forest has covered all traces and the bodies of those laid there were long ago resurrected in the grass and the flowers.

The mountain man became akin to the wild creatures he hunted. It was the woman who clung to small tokens of another world - a broken tortoise comb, pieces of old glass and an occasional silver spoon. It was she who sang the English ballads and told the tales of knights and their ladies in an attempt to bring a touch of grace and beauty to herself and her children.

The wilderness snatched the mountain girl from childhood and hurried her into womanhood almost before she knew what was happening. She was granted a brief time of beauty and burning desire. She mated in the moonlight in forest glens, married in her teens when the Preacher rode by, and as suddenly faded into a drudge and the bearer of children, most of whom died while they were yet babies. One returned to the earth while yet another lay in her womb. It was as if the tiny life had spent a brief time in Heaven and then come back to ease a mother's hunger for her baby. "I am the resurrection and the life: he that believeth in Me, though he were dead, yet shall he live." Each birth was a manifestation of that golden promise.

For the mountain woman mourning came often. It was a time to give vent to weeping and a time to remember that up there was a land brighter than day, where ugliness was washed away and all would be made whiter than snow.

When death touched others than her own she became a professional mourner, a necessary part of all funerals. The service paused to allow her to express the vicarious sadness of all.

Papa and I attended a mountain funeral. A young husband had been shot in a feud. He had five sisters, and after three preachers had spoken for over an hour the mourners lined up to view the remains. The sisters waited their turn. Each remained silent and dry-eyed until she approached the bier. Then with a piercing scream she flung herself upon the corpse. One threw aside the veil and managed to get her arms around the deceased, pulling the body into an almost upright position and showering him with kisses. As the next mourner moved into position she suddenly recovered her calm. It was as if the entire performance had been rehearsed.

Religion was an outlet too. The Camp Meeting was a time for brief repentance and if she couldn't think of an impressive sin to confess she made up something. The professionals fell down on the ground, able to throw themselves into a very real state of catalepsy. They spoke in "the unknown tongue" and those about them strained to get some message from the beyond.

The mountain woman was not immoral but neither was she bound by the mass of man made taboos which frustrated the natural instincts of her lowland sister. She sometimes strayed from her original mate although this was the exception.

Papa told me about one woman who was missing from her home and was later found in a lonesome cabin with a stranger.

"He come up to me at the store," she said. "He had a poke full of candy and he give me some. He had a 'git-tar' and he played a tune and sung me a sad song - I always did love a singin' man."

Hearing her explanation one mountaineer told Papa, "I sure wisht I could git me some of that particular kind of candy!"

The mountain woman was the family physician. She was mid-wife, the brewer of herbs, the maker of poultices. Calmus root, a flag of the *Acorus calmus family* was the base of many remedies.

"What is calmus good for?" my mother asked a mountain woman.

"Well, M'am, hit's good for the belches, the sour belches and the bright."

Some of the cures were born of superstition accompanied by incantations but many were effective too. A wad of cobwebs stopped hemorrhages, and the hepatica, digatalis and foxglove roots provided medicines effective today.

The mountain woman was "neighborly." She could be counted on in time of trouble. She could "birth" a baby (even her own), mend a broken leg and comfort the bereaved. She could "set" a horse, wield an axe, shoot a gun and work the loom, but perhaps her most noteworthy characteristic, that which set her apart from her sisters elsewhere, was her ability to bear the vicissitudes of her hard life in silence. In her black alpaca dress and sun bonnet she sat stiffly in the church, the symbol of the Family. To her husband and her children she was the anchor in time of trouble because of her ability to endure most anything. In the grim reality of her existence all feminine weapons, save one, were swept away. Motherhood was her shield and buckler, the one remaining privilege which marked her from a beast of burden.

The paradoxical characteristics of fanciful dreams and cold realism which have baffled men throughout the ages were present in her too.

Papa told the story of a city couple who climbed the narrow trail to a mountain cabin to get water for their overheated car. They were impressed by the man who met them at the door.

"You don't seem the typical mountain man," the woman said. "What are you doing in this lonesome cabin?"

"I'm a minister of the Gospel," the man replied. "I fell in love with a beautiful yellow-haired girl who played the 'pianner' at the church and I committed a terrible sin with her. I'm up here struggling with a deep repentance and seeking forgiveness."

The woman was touched by his sad story. "Oh, I'm so sorry," she said, "And what about the poor girl, where is she?"

"Oh, she's still down at the church - still playin' the pianner!"

CHAPTER 5

The Charmed Life

Papa led a charmed life!

One perilous adventure followed another, each of which he met with amazing coolness. He was at his best in times of crisis and he escaped serious injury and worse because he was never afraid.

One summer we were camped on the bank of Little River in the foothills of the Smokies. It was a fair-sized stream, turbulent in the shallows and its deep pools were teeming with the cold-water small mouth bass. Papa had decided to paint a heroic-sized picture of the Nativity. He had lumber hauled in by mule team to build a two-tiered scaffold. It had shallow sides and a small overhanging roof. A big piece of canvass rolled down from the top to protect the painting from the weather. A north light filtered through the sycamores which lined both sides of the river bank. Papa painted and fished, fished and painted. Our tent was pitched on a knoll and when we needed supplies we borrowed a horse and buggy from a nearby farm house and drove ten miles to the store.

One moonlight night I was awakened from a sound sleep and found Papa pacing up and down in front of the tent.

"Joe, my tooth is killing me," he said.

We were twenty miles from a dentist. "First thing in the morning we'll drive to Sevierville," I told him.

"Can't stand it that long," Papa said. "I've figured a way to pull it myself."

Despite my protests he set about making preparations. He had me hold the lantern and his shaving mirror. He sterilized his knife, jabbed a hole in his gum at the base of the offending tooth and worked the crook of his trusty buttonhook into the roots. He then tied a piece of heavy fish line to the ring of the hook and fastened a short stick to the free end of the twine. He lay down on the cot and had me shorten the line so it was taut when he drew up his knees. Grabbing the sides of the cot he gave one mighty lunge and out came the tooth. Papa spat a mouthful of blood. Then he took a piece of gauze bandage from the first aid kit, jammed a healthy wad of it into the hole, went back to bed and was soon asleep. I know this because I heard him snoring. As for me, the shock of this fantastic experience kept me awake the rest of the night.

One spring just as the ice was going out Papa and I hitched a ride on the logging road with our gear. They let us off at the mouth of one of the creeks and we hiked up and across "Big Smoky" and pitched camp in a small cove. (In those days practically all the mountains of any size were referred to as "Big Smoky".)

We were having a warm spell and the weather was fine

but the next morning it blew up cold and there was a chill wind which hit us in great gusts. I longed to stay by the campfire but of course Papa was determined to fish. The creek was roaring from the thaw and I spent most of my time scrambling up the side of the mountain to avoid the rushing water. I caught up with Papa about noon but he was on the opposite side of the creek. When I saw him he was down on his hands and knees drinking from a pool which had formed at the base of a high cliff. At that moment a gust of wind blew his hat off and started it toward the rapids. Papa jumped up and almost the instant he did so there was a crack like rifle shot. A huge icicle, ten feet long and the size of a washtub at the base, let loose from the overhanging cliff and buried its needlelike point in the very pool where he had been drinking. It was the dripping from that icicle which had formed the pool. Papa was saved from being decapitated by a chance wind.

I remember a time when we were fishing together in early summer. Papa had climbed out of the river and was working his way along a narrow edge of a cliff to get around a deep pool. I was on the other side and watched him inch along the shelf of the cliff some thirty feet above the water. Just as he reached a sharp bend in the ledge Papa uttered a yell. "Catch my rod," he bellowed and he threw it butt first like a javelin across the narrow gorge. An instant later he plunged feet first from the height into the deep water. After what seemed to me a long time he came floating to the surface and began swimming slowly toward me. When he had dragged himself onto the bank laughing, I exclaimed, "Papa, what in the world did you do that for!"

"Why, just as I stuck my head around that curve in the

cliff I was face to face with the biggest hornets' nest I ever saw. There were hundreds of them and they were looking me right in the eye. If those devils had ever gotten on me I surely believe they would have stung me to death."

One night Papa came home very late, his chin swathed in bandages. His clothes were torn and dirty. He was a sight. "Clifton, what happened? Are you all right?" my mother gasped.

"Oh, I'm fine," Papa said. "I fell into a manhole which some fool had left open at the side of Staub's Theatre — fell clear through to the basement and the first thing that hit was my chin on a two-by-four laid across the coal hole. The doctor said if my head had been turned an inch one way or the other I would have broken my neck. As it was, all he had to do was to take ten stitches in my chin. Fortunately I was pretty relaxed. I'm ashamed to say that I had had a few drinks. "This is one of the few times when I can definitely say that whiskey has been a blessing."

Papa was never an alcoholic but a periodic drinker. When he did drink he entered into it with his usual gusto and got really stoned. Those were the days when drinking was not in its present state of a social grace and we were all deeply ashamed of it. I remember violent arguments between my father and mother and when Papa sobered up he would lecture me at great length on the evils of drink. I developed an almost fanatical prejudice against strong drink and against those who used it — all those except Papa.

My feeling toward my father was paradoxical.

As I crossed the divide between childhood and adolescence I became deeply religious, or perhaps it is more accurate to say that I became an unremitting foe of things considered irreligious. My parents were not staunch church people but revival meetings made a strong impression on me. Drinking, smoking, card playing, even dancing became taboo, and I avoided those who felt otherwise. As I look back on it I can say with all sincerity that I was insufferable.

The discovery that one's own parents are human is apt to come as a shock. In most families it is long delayed and therefore the more painful. In my case the realization came early for Papa made no attempt to appear as something which he was not. He smoked, he drank, he swore and he was not above making a wager. He did these things not only openly but with a certain amount of grace. Some men in telling an off-color story succeed only in making it vulgar while those with the gift are able to make it unobjectionably funny. Papa's sins seemed somehow to strip themselves of their ugliness. He became the one person to whom my uncompromising rules did not apply. In some strange way which even now escapes me, I was able to hate "sin" and love the sinner.

Papa was the only man I have known who went through life with a total disregard for money. We had either great abundance or great need and he adjusted to our fluctuating circumstances without difficulty. When money was plentiful he acted with great largess. He was a handsome and distinguished-looking man and during time of plenty he often decided that he needed new clothes. He would buy not one outfit, but several — a thousand dollars worth. Returning home he would don one of the new suits, sit down at his easel and proceed, in his abstraction, to wipe his brushes on his pants. This drove my mother to tears.

Our lack of financial stability was a source of perennial

worry to my mother and caused most of their quarrels. She often borrowed from my grandfather who was a prosperous Indiana farmer. With this money she would straighten out our accounts.

If Papa had money, you had only to ask and it was yours. "Clifton, you are an easy touch," my mother would say. "Why on earth do you give our money away?"

Papa wanted to paint and of course he wanted to fish but he did not, like Gauguin, desert his family and go his selfish way. No, God bless him, he stuck with it and whatever had to be done to keep us in comfort, he did it. When there were no portraits to paint or when his landscapes did not sell, he painted theatre curtains and even billboards. I used to act as his helper. Many of the boards were painted on location. A metal board with the summer sun reflecting from its surface is one of the hottest places this side of hell. Papa painted beautiful women drinking Coke or eating hamburgers, babies with their bare bottoms turned up to the powder can, dogs, horses, pots of beans or just anything that had to be painted. Only today do I realize what a sacrifice he made!

On one of our forays into the country to repaint a billboard we encountered a band of gypsies camped nearby. The leader approached Papa and asked if he would paint a picture on one of their wagons. "We want a picture of a deer eating grass in the front yard of a house," was the request. (We were neither of us ever able to understand the significance of this scene but Papa delivered exactly what they wanted.) When he had finished, the gypsies began a feverish search for their money which had disappeared from its hiding place. At last it was found and the bills were handed to Papa wringing wet. The children had found the cache and were washing it in the creek!

In addition to what some artists would have considered the humiliating experience of painting billboards, it was necessary for Papa (and later for me, when I became his helper) to join the union. This organization was known as The Painters, Paperhangers and Decorators, of America. Papa had the great gift of taking people as he found them and he made the best of this association.

The meetings of the union could have added chapters to "Robert's Rules of Order" and some of the things which went on were utterly fantastic. I remember one occasion when it was reported that Mayor Guptin of Nashville, Tennessee was having his house painted by "scab" labor (those who did not pay homage to the union). Mayor Guptin also owned the largest shoe store in Nashville. One of the members addressed the Chair, "Mr. Chairman, I move that anybody who buys a pair of shoes from Guptin is a G. D. SOB." The motion was promptly passed unanimously. Papa and I voted for it. These men were good honest, hardworking people. Papa respected them and they often sought his advice, about union strategy.

This is a somewhat roundabout explanation to set the stage for another of Papa's hairbreadth escapes.

Some of his commercial art was painted on the windowless sides of brick buildings. This was done by means of a scaffold hung by two giant hooks from the cornice at the top of the building. The platform on which the painters stood was let down by means of ropes played out in unison to keep the scaffold on an even keel. It was raised and lowered as various portions of the huge pictures were painted.

On this particular occasion Papa had a green helper. It turned out that the poor fellow had never been on a scaffold before and that he suffered from acrophobia as well. As they began their slow descent the helper looked down from the dizzy height of nine stories and in utter panic let go his end of the rope. It somehow caught in one of the floor slats and that was all that saved them from being dashed to death. The scaffold was now almost perpendicular with Papa hanging onto the high end and his helper clinging to the lower end, his feet clawing for a foothold on emptiness. He was in a state of complete shock, unable to do anything but cling desperately to the caught rope.

Papa talked to him, at first soothingly. He promised him that he was not going to fall and that if he did exactly as he was told they would soon be safe on the ground. Then he began to give the man commands in a matter-of-fact voice; he told him where to fix his eyes, what to do with his right leg and then his left leg. The helper obeyed as if mesmerized. He got his hands on the rope, he pulled as Papa lowered. Slowly the platform righted itself and they began their painful descent. At last they reached the ground and the inevitable crowd which gathers to watch bridge jumpers and to view the tragedies of their fellowmen, set up a cheer. The helper fainted. Papa sent for another helper, pulled the stage back up nine stories and finished the day's work.

That poor fellow never forgot the man who had saved his life. For many years afterward he would take Papa fishing. He did not fish himself but he would wait patiently to drive him back home at the end of the day.

Papa owned wilderness land in Arkansas and during my early years he made frequent trips to the settlement of

"Marked Tree" to fish, hunt and trap in the "Sunk Lands." I remember a cap my mother made for me out of the hide of a bobcat with the stubby tail hanging down the back, and I recall the mink fur piece which Papa had fashioned for her.

The Sunk Lands of Arkansas were alive with fish and game. It was mostly uninhabited country, dark and dangerous, and it was risky to venture far without a guide. The wilderness abounded with wild pigs. To hunt in this domain you must first own land and if you bought a brood sow and turned her loose you were entitled to shoot pork.

Papa got lost in the swamp. He was in a dugout canoe with a gun and fishing rod. He wouldn't starve to death but there were other dangers. These lowlands were infested with hordes of biting insects and the heavy miasma of swamp fever and malaria hung over the land. Then there were the snakes, the deadly cottonmouth or water moccasin. These venomous creatures hung on the limbs of low-hanging trees and bushes and Papa said that often his boat would brush them off so that they writhed at his feet until they found their way over the side helped by the paddle. The nights were cold and he had to sleep in the narrow confines of the boat for it was hard to find the little hillocks of dry land and then there were many dangers ashore. It became a question of how long he would be able to stand the rigors of the swamp for there seemed no way out.

In the afternoon of the fourth day he caught a faraway cry which seemed human. He could not get the boat through in that direction and he abandoned it and began his slow progress on foot, sometimes up to his armpits in the water. At last he emerged onto high ground and discovered a cabin. He called out but there was no answer. Pushing through the cabin door he found a small group of women and children seated on the floor around a dead man. They were wailing and crying and from the look of the corpse they had been at it for some time. They were apparently afraid to touch the deceased.

Papa closed the man's eyes and did what he could to prepare him for burial. He dug a shallow grave beside the cabin and laid him in it. He spent the night outside and in the morning a twelve year old boy led him out of the swamp.

Papa's miraculous luck had held. He had been saved by a dead man!

CHAPTER 6

"On Top Of Old Smoky"

Sixteen peaks of the Great Smokies rise to an elevation of 6000 feet. Clingman's Dome (6421) is the highest point east of the Rockies but Mt. LeConte (elevation 6593') is the "tallest" from its base. LeConte is forest clad. Virgin mixed hardwoods grow on the lower and intermediate slopes, virgin red spruce and fir (balsam) adorn the top stretches.

This old mountain I know well. From its top I have watched gentle sunsets and viewed the thundering dawn. Papa and I scratched our way up its ancient surface on foot and I have also negotiated it after a fashion on horseback. I say "after a fashion" for I remember being bucked off my mount several times when swarms of yellow jackets needled the poor animal into a frenzy.

Others have climbed the mountain under far less auspicious conditions than I. The champion was a fellow, friend of Papa's, who took his old Mother up and down strapped to his back in a chair!

"Eulis, I want to see the sunrise top of Old Smoky afore I die," she told him at the age of 92. "You know I can't git up and down by myself. How do you figure I could do it?"

Eulis cut the legs off a split-bottom chair and strapped the old lady in as comfortable position as possible, covered her with a big blanket and set out for the top. He made it all right and they spent the night before a roaring fire in the herder's cabin at the top. They watched the sun come up and then started down. "Goin' down was a mite harder than goin' up," he told Papa. "In the steep places I had to back down. Sure wisht I had wore me a pair of gloves!"

The high peaks of the Smokies are for the most part bare of trees and covered with a variety of thick grasses. These "balds," as they are called, are a strange phenomenon, not cleared by man. The mountaineers took their sheep and cattle to these grazing lands in the summer and built rough log huts with huge fireplaces. Long before the hostels, these huts sheltered many a weary traveler and no doubt saved the lives of early settlers caught in blizzards crossing the mountains.

Late one fall Papa and I climbed the mountain planning to spend the night in the herder's cabin. Half way to the top it began to snow. The wind blew strongly from the North. The snow was wet and festooned every limb and twig. The north side of the trail was enveloped in a white blanket and across from it the flaming colors of autumn were in their full glory.

By the time we reached the summit we were in a blizzard and we had a hard time keeping to the trail. The biting wind smashed into us and we struggled desperately to reach shelter. At last we found the cabin. Smoke was rising from the chimney and we kicked the door open to find a group of men

"ON TOP OF OLD SMOKY"

huddled about the fire. They were hikers from Asheville, over on the North Carolina side, and they had made the top a good two hours ahead of us — fortunately in time to accumulate a huge pile of firewood. Men and boys, they were twelve.

We pooled our food and had a good supper together. As the night wore on the storm increased. We were all pretty tuckered out from the climb, but it was so cold that sleep was impossible. Besides, there wasn't enough room in the cabin for all of us to lie down. We pulled up the rough benches to the fire — one bench in front, the other directly behind it - and rotated from back to front. When the front seven got warm they changed places with those behind them. We melted snow in front of the fire for drinking water. Sitting on the back row I reached down for the dipper to get a drink. The whole bucket came off the floor. The water had frozen solid!

We sat around with blankets over our shoulders getting better acquainted and "yarning." Papa had the best stories and the most, too.

One of our new acquaintances was a dentist. Under a Government health program he had visited a number of mountain communities to examine the teeth of the children. "I examined a big buxom girl about sixteen. 'You have the most perfect teeth I have ever seen,' I told her. One of the incisors was missing. 'How did you lose that tooth?' I asked her. 'Hit got to hurtin' one night and Pap took a ten-penny nail and knocked it out!' "

Another was a doctor who told about removing a huge cyst, or wen, from the top of a mountaineer's head. "When he found out I was a doctor he said, 'Doc, I'd be obliged to you if you would cut this damn thing offen my head. Got so's I can't hardly git my hat on.' I had brought along a small instrument case. In it was a hypodermic but no drugs. "Yes, I can take it off without much trouble but it's going to hurt. Don't know if you will be able to stand it.' 'Oh I kin accommodate pain considerable, Doc. Don't worry about me, Just cut hit off.' He sat down in a chair and gripped the lower rungs. 'Git me a big chew of tobaccy,' he told his woman. I injected hot water at the base of the growth, cleaned out the sebaceous material and peeled it off. He never even grunted!"

Papa told about a funeral he had attended for old Uncle Enoch who lived in one of the distant coves. The peculiar thing about the funeral was the fact that there was nobody in the pine box which the pall bearers carried down the aisle. Uncle Enoch was sitting in the front row of the church very much alive. Three preachers spoke at length about the sterling qualities of the patriarch, interrupted frequently by suggestions and downright criticism from Enoch when the ceremony didn't go to suit him. "He's been having these rehearsals for the last five years," Papa told them. "They are big events and people from all around come to the funeral laden with food. Looks as if Uncle Enoch will outlast many of his mourners."

This gathering of mountain folk reminded somebody to tell about the Ramp Festival. The Ramp is a wild leek, akin to the onion of the *Liliaceae* (lily) family. Its potent flavor is known far and wide in the mountains and it is said that those who have eaten of it announce their coming at a

"ON TOP OF OLD SMOKY"

greater distance than a skunk can be detected Matter of fact, one whiff of the breath of a Ramp eater has an almost anesthesic effect upon those around him.

The talk turned to mountain justice and Papa told about the mountaineer who was guiding him through a remote section. They spied a cabin perched on stilts high on the mountain side. "Killed a man up thar t'other month," the man said.
"What did they do to you?" Papa asked.
"Nothin," was the reply, "I war shootin' at his brother."

Someone mentioned the quaint names the mountain people gave their children. They needed a great variety for their large families. In the early days ten to fourteen offspring was quite common. Biblical names of course were in the majority with a preference for the high-sounding ones — Zebulun, Jethro, Leviticus, Nicodemus. Nobody bothered to pronounce such names but contracted them to the first syllable or called the victim by some descriptive nickname. Then there were such names as Doc, Judge, Squire, General, Captain, Sargeant, Sheriff and even Mister. The mother, who always named her children had someone in mind who bore these titles.

I ventured the story of a child whom my Mother met at a cross-roads store in the Mountains. "What is your boy's name," she asked his mother. "Gooey," was the answer. "I have never heard that name before." said Mama. "How do you spell it?"
"Why we spell hit G-U-Y."

At last we ran out of stories or the urge to tell them, and someone dug out a paperback detective story from his knapsack and we all read it at the same time. How can fourteen people read one small book simultaneously? Papa showed us the way — you just tear out a page at a time and pass it to the man on your left. Fourteen pages equal fourteen readers!

The next morning the North Carolinians went down the eastern side of the mountain, and Papa and I headed west. Halfway down there was no snow and the Autumnal colors blazed forth in all their glory. I shall always remember that night on Old Smoky. It seemed that high atop the mountain we were on another planet. Oh the healing Balm of Nature's Solitude! Man's soul shrinks when "the earth is too much with us." He needs to escape the tentacles of civilization to discover himself and if he finds no comfort in nature he suffers from a sickness that is not temporal.

That night it suddenly became clear to me what Papa meant when he spoke of the forest as his church and the mountain as his altar.

CHAPTER 7

Life on the Ohio

Papa was born in the town of Leavenworth, Indiana on the bank of the Ohio in the year 1858. It was the Mark Twain era and like Tom Sawyer, the River flowed through his boyhood. Here he began his career as a fisherman for the mighty Ohio teemed with piscatorial opportunity. Channel catfish and sturgeon were abundant and game fish abounded in the tributaries. There were gar, mud and snapping turtles, mink, muskrat and otter; ducks and geese. A myriad of water birds used it as a highway on their migratory flights. He remembered great clouds of the now extinct passenger pigeon so numerous that they literally obscured the sun and the land became dark with their passing.

At age twelve he got his first set of paints, water colors. The town's richest man lived in a big house overlooking the river. His hobby was birds and he actually had an aviary. Papa and fellow conspirators proceeded to create from a white farmyard duck a creature of brilliant magnificence.

They whittled his bill to a point and then Papa went to work on him with his paints. When he was through, nature had not conceived such a varicolored and gaudy creature. They took it to the house on the hill claiming that they had captured it on a sandbar. The old man who suffered from myopia paid them the unheard sum of five dollars and turned it loose among his other treasures. After the first hard rain the duck regained its normal insignificance and Papa was called on to return his ill-gotten gains.

He became a successful hunter of the elusive goose. To get a goose with a rifle required great stalking skill for geese never stop to rest or feed without posting a lookout. "The goose can smell a man at a great distance," Papa told me. "He must not only be approached downwind but I always took a bath and changed to clean underwear before I went hunting."

One winter morning Papa took a shot at the leader of a "V" shaped flight of Canada geese. "They must have been over a mile high and I had no idea of hitting anything. I had a 30-30. I took my sight well ahead of the flock and pulled the trigger. To my suprise I saw the leader falter and then start the long descent. I found him down river a good half mile from where I stood. He was split in half, frozen solid." Thus Papa produced the first deepfreeze goose anywhere.

As he grew older he and his companions roamed the banks of the river by night. They built huge driftwood fires on the sandy bars and roasted chickens which they pilfered from hen houses in the vicinity. One of the boys was the rich man's son. His personality did not recommend him to the gang. On a particular night he brought along his colored slave to barbecue the chickens and suggested that they raid the coop of a "widow-woman" nearby. Papa and another were chosen by lot to get the chickens but instead of going to the widow's house they visited the boy's home and with great stealth secured a half dozen of his prize chickens. While plucking the fowls the colored man said, "Marsa George, I do declare this little red rooster looks exactly like yourn." The rest of the crowd ate with gusto.

There were clandestine cock fights in barns by lantern light and substantial sums were wagered on the outcome. Papa had an old dominique rooster whose foot had been frozen; the toes were missing and he hobbled around on a big knot the size of a walnut. Now a blooded fighting cock's humor is considerably agitated if he is allowed to make a kill before the real fight. A neighbor, the owner of an expensive fighting cock, slipped through the barnyard fence of my grandfather's house and tossed his prize in front of the old rooster. Almost immediately they joined in battle. The fighting cock had on steel spurs and it looked like no contest but the old rooster leaped high in the air and by sheer luck brought that stump of his bad leg right down with full force on the cock's skull. He must have weighed three times as much as his opponent and the force of the blow put an end to the career of the professional. Then the cock's owner took out after the old rooster, bent on killing him. That brought Papa out of the house. "I had to whip that man to keep him from killing my old rooster," he told me.

Papa had quite a career as a country fighter. He claimed that it was wished on him.

He was not a big man — about five feet ten inches and weighed 170 pounds — but he was all muscle and bone even to his dying day and was quick as a cat.

In those days every river community had its town "bully," anxious to prove his prowess. It was something like the old

West except they used fists instead of guns. On a Sunday afternoon Papa was confronted by one of these hearties from down river. "Just couldn't avoid a fight," he told me. "The street was deep in mud and he came for me in the middle of it. He must have been a good three inches over six feet. I circled, holding him off, until I got to the plank sidewalk which was two feet above the road. I jumped onto the walkway and as he lunged I caught him square on the jaw and he went down in the mud and never got up. That was the end of the fight.

"The word spread how the 'Bully' of Leavenworth had whipped the 'Bully' from Cannelton and from time to time various men from other towns came to try me.

"Most of these heroes were big men and it was rough going with no holds barred. Boxing skill had not yet made its appearance and they came in swinging wildly. Often the fights ended up on the ground where you had a good chance of getting an eye gouged out. These fights took the place of the professional sports of today and the crowds that gathered round loved it. I knew if one of those giants ever got his arms around me, I was done for. The only thing that saved me was my speed and I perfected some fancy footwork which not only kept me out of reach but also served to enrage my opponents and make them throw caution to the winds. I got the name of a pretty dirty fighter. It was all right to bite, scratch and kick but to sidestep a blow was something else.

"I did the best I could. I won some and I lost a few."

Papa told me about these encounters with the injured air of a man who had been pushed into them but he didn't fool me for a minute. It was plain as the nose on your face that Papa loved to fight.

LIFE ON THE OHIO

Papa had a variety of occupations before he dedicated himself to Art and Fishing. He read Law in a Judge's office and became Assistant Prosecuting Attorney for the State of Indiana, appeared briefly on the stage in a play called "Lady of Lyons" and taught classes in Penmanship at various "Academies."

He struck up a warm friendship with James Whitcomb Riley, the Hoosier poet. They roamed about together, Papa writing poetry and Riley trying to paint. I have some of Papa's published verses. They are mostly about nature and followed the musical iambic pentameter of the day They are not very good.

After a time each man turned to the thing he could do best and Riley became a household word in the Middle West

My mother, ten years younger than he, was in one of Papa's Penmanship classes. "I went out to her father's farm one Sunday afternoon. She gave me a glass of cold buttermilk from the springhouse and I kissed her," Papa said. "You know, after that every time I went to see her she met me at the door with a glass of buttermilk."

Papa began his full time career in art as a portrait painter. He shared a studio with a photographer. One day a man who was a stranger to Papa, came to visit the photographer. A few days before, a very homely woman had come in to have her picture taken. "Beyond a doubt she was the ugliest woman I had ever seen," Papa said. "It was unbelievable. Well, this stranger and I got to talking about one thing and another and I told him that I wanted him to see the ugliest woman in the world. Tom Tyler, the photographer, and I

53

searched high and low but we simply couldn't find that picture.

"When the man had gone Tom wiped his brow and said, 'Whew, that was a close call! I'm glad that I managed to get hold of that picture before you did. The ugly woman is that man's favorite sister'."

In those days chewing tobacco was a favorite male vice. The "readymade" cigaret was unknown and plug tobacco was a necessary part of the equipment of many who considered themselves "He men." The cuspidor or "garboon" was a standard part of the furnishings in offices and public places and the poor marksmanship of those addicted to this filthy habit was evidenced by the brown splatterings on the walls and baseboards where these receptacles were placed. If many missed, there were also the experts. Contests at great distances were held and the more accomplished marksmen were actually able to spit a "curve." An obstruction was placed in front of the spittoon and the experts could hit it with a burst of saliva which "broke" toward the target at the proper instant. The spittoons were mostly made of brass and gave forth the ring of a bell when struck solidly.

Men of the so-called "lower classes" chewed openly but the "nobility" tried to conceal it from the ladies who took a dim view of the pastime. Many swains carried a small wad of chewing tobacco concealed somewhere in the back recesses of their mouths and would wait for an undetected moment to expectorate. If you noticed a man making furtive movements in an attempt to disengage himself you would know what was the matter with him. Failing to get away, he simply swallowed!

In my day at the University of Tennessee many of the

students chewed tobacco for smoking was forbidden on the campus and linemen on the football team carried large chaws into battle where they were wont to spit in the eye of opponents in an attempt to get them to strike the first blow and thus be ejected from the game. A somewhat incongruous situation existed at Tennessee regarding smoking. We were lectured at length on the evils of cigarettes (how right they were has only lately become apparent) while down at the experimental farm they were doing their darndest to develop better cigarette tobaccos. The badge of the law student was a chew in cheek. You simply had to chew tobacco if you studied law - otherwise you would be ostracized.

I remember one "Toots" McCoy, a fraternity brother of mine. Toots was a prodigious chewer. He was a member of the Glee Club and sang a mean tenor. One night we gave a concert in old Science Hall at the University. The program consisted of choral, quartet and solo numbers and Toots was down for a solo. The performers were seated behind a large screen on the platform and came out as their numbers were announced. "When am I on, boys?" Toots asked. "Do I have time for a chew?"

We assured him that he did and he took a large bite and began to dehydrate it with enthusiasm. Somebody slipped around and tipped off the student who was announcing the program. We let Toots get the chew in a state of full activity and then came the call, "We will now have a tenor solo by Mr. Harold McCoy."

With that, a couple of us hustled Toots to his feet and literally pushed him out from behind the screen and in front of the audience. McCoy was a boy of vast resources. "Excuse me, folks," he said and calmly spit the wad of tobacco into his hand and tossed it into the footlights. He then proceeded to sing like a bird. When the last sweet note died away the crowd arose as one man and gave him an ovation.

The leading plug tobacco of that day was "Climax." Huge billboards extolling its virtues dotted the landscape. One showed a farmer with a huge bulge in his cheeck. "It ain't toothache, it's CLIMAX," the sign read.

After he got out of college Toots took a job with Climax calling on the trade. He used to visit the fraternity house and tell of his experiences. "Why it's the finest chewing tobacco in the world!" he said. "Not long ago I was on the train to Chattanooga. I had a big chew in my mouth and was looking around for a place to spit just as we pulled into Loudon. The window was open and I let fly when the train slowed down. There was a big man standing at the end of the platform and I hit him right in the face. Well sir, that fellow hopped aboard and went down the aisle pointing at every man he came to. 'Was that you spit on me?' he yelled. I tell you I was scared to death. I knew when he got to me the expression on my face would give me away.

"There he stood, right over me and before he could get the question out I started apologizing, but he stopped me — 'That's all right, son,' he said. 'I just wanted to know what brand you air chewin'.'"

Papa didn't chew tobacco but one day he had a toothache and the photographer gave him a small sliver to hold in his mouth to "ease the pain." Papa kept asking for tobacco, even after the tooth had been pulled. One day Tyler said, "Kip, go out and buy your own tobacco. You have got the habit."

Papa was working in pastels. I can remember those delicate colored chalks and the long wooden boxes which held them. Portraits done in pastels had an ethereal porcelain-like quality. They were very delicate and glass was always placed over the picture to preserve it.

As the artist worked, he had to keep blowing away the pastel dust which accumulated on the picture. Papa would expectorate in the cuspidor, placed conveniently on his right, and then blow on the picture. . . . You've guessed it — one day in his concentration he reversed the process; he blew into the spittoon and spit on the portrait. He ruined it and that was the last time he ever chewed tobacco.

Papa married Mama in the month of June 1899 and I came along in December of 1900. The carefree bachelor, artist, sportman was now a family man and he took it in his stride. As I said before, he never shirked his responsibility but he didn't let it bother him either. He continued to paint and hunt and fish and when the larder ran low, he turned his hand to whatever he could with no complaint.

If I had to reach the full maturity of the sixties to appreciate my father, it is also true that I did not understand the trials and tribulations that Mama faced in her marriage.

Leora Weathers was the daughter of Joseph Weathers, a prosperous farmer who returned from the War between the States and through a provident nature and the backbreaking work of the farm built a happy and comfortable life for his family.

Grandpa was an officer in the 23rd Indiana Cavalry. He was a great horseman and got his pick of horses. He chose all blacks and the Company must have been a brave sight. In the Tennessee campaign his horse was shot out from under him and he appropriated a big saddle mule from one of the farms in the path of the advancing army. "Many of my men wanted to give me their horses," he said, "but I stuck to the mule. The roads for the most part were quagmires and that big mule plowed through them with no trouble at all. He was the finest mount I ever rode."

Grandpa was captured and imprisoned in the house of General Zollicofer in Nashville. I have been in the very room where he was held prisoner. He escaped and rejoined his Company in Georgia. When the war was over his men presented him with a very handsome engraved sword. When Grandpa got back he sawed it in half and used the pieces for corn knives.

From the rolling acres of rich Indiana bottom land and the security of order and plenty, Mama became a wandering gypsy. We lived in many places. I was in and out of schools from Indiana to Georgia. Papa went where he could find a market for his talents and he always favored locations where the game was plentiful and the fishing good. Sometimes Mama refused to move and he went alone but he always came back. Mama held the family together and Papa was well content to let her do it. She was a small frail woman and had four major operations but her spirit was indomitable. She lived to the age of 94.

CHAPTER 8

Home Was a Place of Laughter

I had a happy childhood.

Papa's sense of humor never failed him. He had the rare gift of finding life not only interesting but extremely funny. He was able to extract the humorous from the most serious and seemingly disastrous events which befell us and as often as not he himself was the butt of his jokes. He was a brilliant conversationalist and was famous for his stories. These were all the more interesting because they were for the most part true.

To be sure everything was not always good temper and harmony, but it was either one way or another; there was never any long drawn out grumpiness. Papa was not a sulker. If something displeased him, you knew it immediately.

When Papa got worked up he could swear in a most magnificent manner. He could swear in both English and German and he also knew expressive Indian phrases which he had picked up from the Cheyenne and Blackfoot tribes when he hunted and fished with them in Wyoming and the Dakotas.

I have always thought that the Scriptures should have differentiated between the many forms of profanity rather than to have condemned them all. Papa's swearing did not seem like blasphemy; actually it sounded more like a reverent recognition of the Infinite, an attempt to communicate and to call down the wrath of the Omnipotent on inanimate objects which got in his way. Papa never swore at any of us although he often cussed his own stupidity.

When I speak of Papa's familiarity with the German language I think of Stephanie. During one of our more prosperous times we had a full-time maid who lived with us. Stephanie was right off the boat and spoke only halting English. I was fascinated by her German and wanted very much to learn to talk to her in her native tongue.

At that time my brother Frank was on the way and they wanted to break me of the habit of climbing into bed with my mother. I didn't like the idea and resisted sleeping in the room with Stephanie. "Joe, the way to learn to speak German is to sleep with Stephanie," Papa told me.

One night we gave a big dinner party and while Stephanie was serving, Papa spoke to her in German whereupon I pointed an accusing finger at him and declared, "Papa, I know what you've been doing. You've been sleeping with Stephanie!"

Papa roared with laughter. It was up to Mama to attempt the somewhat involved explanation.

But Mama had a sense of humor, too, and it tided us over many a rough spot. We had a lot of family jokes.

One night Mama, who was a fine cook, baked what she thought was a cinnamon coffee ring. As it turned out in the poor light of the cabinet, she had mistaken the word "Cincinnati" for "Cinnamon." The tin contained ground cloves put up by a Cincinnati concern. The aroma, once the cake began to rise, was overpowering. Mama wrapped the mess up in a fancy box. She put a note inside which read:

Dear John,

 I am sending you one of Emma's famous coffee rings. She has won blue ribbons at the fair with this cake and I know all of you will find it delicious.

Mama sent me up to Hill Street, a busy thoroughfare, and had me drop the box on the sidewalk. It was great fun to speculate on just who had found it and what they said about "Emma's" cooking!

Neither Mama nor Papa was what is termed religious. Papa was outspoken in his opinions. I believe he classed himself as an Agnostic, an evil sounding word with which many an honest man has been damned. Papa was the most honest man I have ever known and the hypocrisy of some of the staunch church members he knew sickened him. No doubt this was a poor reason for staying out of the church but it must be remembered that the churches of his youth were stilted and uncompromising and had little use for those who were inclined to ask questions about their dogmas. You either swallowed it whole or they condemned you to outer darkness.

Papa was an admirer of Robert Ingersoll, the iconoclast of his day. "They claim that Ingersoll was 'converted' on his deathbed," he told me, "but that is a lie circulated by his hypocritical enemies. They worked on him hard in his weakened condition but he held out to the very end."

On the other hand Papa was a man of reverence and I am sure that he believed in God. He simply found it impossible to accept the various and mundane descriptions of Him and to swallow the many acts attributed to His wrathful power. I remember his scorn when two boys who had gone boating on Sunday were overturned and drowned and it was said that God in his wrath at the desecration of the Sabbath had Himself upset the boat. Papa was full of the milk of human kindness. I would say that he was a worshiper of Nature which is perhaps as near as most of us are able to come to an understanding of the manifestations of a Higher Power.

My brother and I attended Sunday School and church but it was Mama who took us. Papa seldom went along. The Methodist Church where we were members got a new minister who was long-winded and spoke at great length about his travels. "What do you think of our new minister, Mrs. Long?" a member of the congregation asked her.

"Well," my mother said, "I must say that each Sunday I am literally worn out at the end of the service for I am dragged all over the Holy Land and adjoining territory. I do hope the next one we get has never been to the Holy Land or if he has, that he has been there twice."

A neighbor said, "Mrs. Long, you have such a talented family. Your husband is an artist and your youngest son is an artist and Joe is a writer. What do you do?"

"Why, I live with them," Mama replied.

I have never forgotten the lessons Papa taught me. He had a great gift of driving home his point. He never lectured me. His orders were issued firmly and in a few words and he never humiliated me.

My brother Frank inherited Papa's artistic skill. He was a much better draftsman than Papa and began to indicate this ability at a very early age. I don't think I was jealous but I smarted under my total inability to draw. I was in the fourth grade and we were having an exhibit of drawings. Papa was sketching the cover for a sports magazine. I can see it today; the catcher squatting down behind the plate, the umpire towering over his head and the batter tense and determined, waiting for the pitch. I got a piece of semitransparent paper, laid it down over the sketch and painfully traced the outlines. Then I added a few amateurish scribbles of my own and turned it in at school. How Papa found out about it I'll never know but I remember sitting with him on the back steps of our house. I was thoroughly ashamed of what I had done but he approached the episode with such kindness and understanding that it took on the aspect of a mistake instead of a major sin. I did have to tell my teacher what I had done and that was hard to do but when it was over I felt very good about it.

One afternoon Papa took me to the Fair. There were huge crowds at the ticket windows. The street car made a complete circle of the fairgrounds before stopping at the ticket booths. At the back of the grounds there was a big hole in the bottom of the fence and men and boys poured off the open car and proceeded to wriggle under the fence. Papa and I were among them. Of course I enjoyed slipping in immensely and kept remarking on how smart we were. As we approached the main gate to go home Papa said, "Joe, here is the money for our tickets. You take it to the booth and tell the man that to save time we went in through the fence."

Papa had a mind like a steel trap and he was at his best making split-second decisions during times of emergency.

One day we were walking home from town across a high wooden bridge. A single streetcar track ran so close to the one board walk that pedestrians had to stand near the rail to keep from getting hit. I was a long way ahead of Papa and so engrossed in whatever occupied my attention that I was oblivious to the streetcar which was bearing down on me. Papa took in the situation at a glance. He was afraid to call out for fear I would step right in front of the oncoming streetcar. Instead he gave a sharp whistle, rushed to the rail and pointed to the creek below. I immediately dashed over to the safe side in my eagerness to see what had attracted his attention just as the car sped past. A short time afterward a boy was struck and killed in almost that very spot.

One fall Papa borrowed a canvas boat and we went duck hunting on the Little Tennessee. We had expected to make the mouth of the river about dark and board the train for home but Papa was never able to keep a strict schedule and dark found us a good ten miles from our destination. "We can't travel this river in the dark," Papa said, "We'll just pull into the bank and go to sleep."

About that time it began to drizzle. Papa found an overhanging rock and we hollowed out a place in the leaves and burrowed in like a couple of bears. In a few minutes Papa was sound asleep but I lay awake listening to the strange sounds of the woods and the river. The next morning we found enough dry wood to build a fire and we cooked one of the ducks but we had no salt and it tasted very flat. We put the boat in and paddled downstream. Around a bend we saw men and women digging potatoes in a distant field. "I've just got to have a cup of coffee, Joe," Papa said.

"Well, I don't see how you're going to get one until we reach the railroad."

"I want you to go up to that field and ask one of those women to make me a cup," Papa said.

I protested and he insisted so there was nothing to do but go up and ask. I was only thirteen and I tell you I felt pretty silly. Papa didn't tell me what to say and so I had to improvise as I climbed the hill. The woman was very nice. I followed her about a half mile to the farmhouse and waited while she brewed the coffee. Then I carried it back in a mason jar and Papa drank about a quart. I then took the jar back and offered her a quarter which she refused.

Mama had expected us home the night before and when we got to the little railroad station they told us the Sheriff of Loudon county was out looking for us. Papa called Mama. He seemed very much surprised that she had been concerned. "Why Leora, you should have known that we were all right."

"I knew no such a thing," Mama said. "If you want to go off by yourself and sleep in the rain on river banks, I suppose I can't stop you but the next time you leave Joe at home."

Life with Papa was often harrowing but never dull. I soon got used to moving and our fluid existence did not disturb me. It is only now that I begin to understand what went on back stage. This understanding makes me doubly grateful to both of my parents for the happy childhood made possible by their sacrifice. If I ever lie down on the couch of a psychiatrist I will have absolutely nothing to tell him about my early life which will throw any light on whatever is eating me.

I have had as hard a time as most keeping the Ten Commandments . . . nine of them, that is, for "Honor Thy

Father and Thy Mother" posed no problem. My measure of health, success and happiness I freely ascribe to what God gave me through heredity and what Mama and Papa gave me by teaching and example. This precious inheritance far outweighs my own small accomplishment.

During my tenth year my Mother, Brother and I visited my Uncle "Doc," a prominent surgeon, in Indiana. One afternoon a messenger arrived with a telegram for Mama. "Clifton J. Long passed away at 10 a.m. this morning." It was signed by someone unfamiliar to us.

Even today the memory of this time lingers in my mind. I can see myself sitting on the curb in front of my Uncle's house. It was a time of sadness and disbelief. My suffering was unbearable. I remember too how one of my small friends who had lost his Father came to sit beside me and how he tried to comfort me.

"There is something strange about this message," my Uncle said. "I just don't believe it!" In those days long-distance 'phone calls were in the primitive stage but after several hours Uncle got through to our home. There was no answer. We waited through the long night and the next morning it was decided to call a neighbor. The Misses Hedgecock lived in a fine old mansion near our home. They were lovely women, members of an old Tennessee family and circumspect with the primness which characterizes females who enjoy the state of single blessedness.

Miss Helen offered to hurry up the hill to our home while my Uncle held the 'phone. Papa told about it later — "I was in the shower and answered the door in my dressing gown, totally unaware of my own demise — Miss Helen threw her arms around me and showered me with kisses —

'Oh, Mr. Long,' she gushed 'I was never so glad to see anyone in my life!' "

The mystery was never entirely cleared up although there was a hint of what may have happened. About a week later two representatives of a small southern Life Insurance company called on Papa and tried to sell him insurance. The day after it dawned on Papa that the telegram might have been used to soften up their prospects. The company had no local office and Papa was never able to find the men. I have always been glad that they escaped for I am sure Papa would not have waited for the law to take its course!

CHAPTER 9

Pace Whitestone

Although fishing was his first love, Papa was a great hunter too.

He shot grizzlies in Colorado, antelope in Wyoming, moose in Canada and wild boar and bobcat in Arkansas. He was a crack shot with rifle and shotgun and he delighted in hunting the southern bobwhite or quail as they are called in the South.

He was the greatest dog trainer I ever heard about. All of his dogs were great retrievers with tender mouths and they would lay a bird right in your hand with hardly a feather out of place. He always hunted with a pair of dogs, one to range and find the coveys and the other to painstakingly ferret out the singles, once the flock had been scattered.

He chose names for his dogs that were easily called in the field: Doc, Smock, Bango, Jack, but the greatest of these was a dog named Pace.

Pace was the joint property of Papa and a sportsman

named Tom Pace. They paid a great deal of money for the pup for he was the son of Prince Whitestone, a Canadian Irish Setter who had won the National Field Trials at Grand Junction, Tennessee. The dog was shipped South but almost from the day of his arrival he had one spell of sickness after another. First it was distemper and then the mange. He lost all of his hair and he was a most pathetic sight — skin and bones, and naked as a jaybird. Papa took him from one Vet to another but none of them seemed to be able to do anything for him. Finally Tom Pace said, "Mr. Long, I've spent my last dollar on that poor dog. I'm through and what's left of him is yours — that is if you want him."

Well, of course Papa did want him and he began a series of experiments which took place in our basement next to the furnace. Mama complained of the odor but she put up with it. Evenings my brother and I would go down to see poor little Pace. We would hold his head and pet him and although he seemed to appreciate it, he just couldn't be coaxed into getting on his feet. Papa fed him raw eggs and warm milk. He poured it down his throat and made him swallow by holding his nose.

This went on for most of the winter. When spring came Pace was able to move about the basement and he began eating a little by his own efforts. All of a sudden his hair started to grow back and by the time summer came he had the most glorious coat you ever saw. The "feathers" on his legs were a good three inches long and his tail waved in the air like a banner. Now he was out in the run and Papa was soon taking him to the open fields for his training.

From the beginning he showed the skill and stamina of his illustrious father. Once off the leash he sprang into action which consisted of heading for the next county. He disdained anything short of a full covey and once he had found it he was off again, content to let the other dogs pick up the leavings. He was hard to follow on foot. Many times we would find him far, far away from where he had been put down, frozen stiff in a "point" or creeping slowly forward, following the quail as they tried to escape on the ground.

One day Tom Pace came to see Papa and there stood the beautiful pup in all his glory. "Where in the world did you get that dog, Mr. Long? He looks like one of the Whitestone strain."

"Why that's your namesake, Tom", my father said. "That's old Pace."

"Pace is a field trial dog if I ever saw one," Papa said. "I'm going to enter him at Grand Junction." I was fifteen and it was decided that I should take him to the Trials.

We put Pace in his handsome traveling box. He rode in the baggage car and I shuttled back and forth throughout the journey to keep him company. I was a very important young man!

Last year I visited Grand Junction and despite the passage of some fifty years the place looks much the same as it did to that excited boy of long ago. You can see the old carriages in the barn museum. They met the trains to haul men and dogs to the five thousand acre plantation where the meet was held. The handlers rode mules behind their dogs. A brace of dogs — competing against each other — would be put down, the judges following to tally up the points.

Pace was still a pup but in those days they held a derby for two year olds and this was his event. The going was rough, across stony ground and through briar patches. Some of the dogs had to quit because of sore and bleeding feet but Pace was going full tilt at the end of the second day and by that time it had narrowed down to our dog and a pointer from Canada — one of the puppies of another grand champion, Manitoba Rap. As the long day drew to a close the dogs were even in the number of coveys they had found. I didn't know what the judge would say but I thought Pace showed more style than his opponent. We came to a deep ravine through which flowed a creek. Both dogs plunged in at about the same time but the pointer stopped to drink. Pace just hit it a lap on the way through and when he topped the hill beyond, he froze into a magnificent point and that was the ball game. You can imagine my pride when I boarded the train that night with the big cup under my arm!

One day Papa came home from a fishing trip with a string of bass and a little English setter puppy. He had found the dog at a mountain cabin and had bought it for five dollars. The mountaineer had declared that it was a "full-blooded bird dog" although of course he had no registration papers. Papa named him Jack and he grew into a big powerful animal and turned out to be one of the best hunting dogs in the string. Jack had all the markings of the bird dog but he had a thick bull neck and heavy powerful legs. When we went hunting we usually took along at least four dogs and we would hunt a pair, then let them rest for a day and use the other two. One day we put Jack in a farmer's barn where we were staying and left early the next morning with the brace of fresh dogs. After we had been gone about an hour here comes Jack! He had climbed the ladder to the hay loft and jumped out of the loft window. When there was hunting to be done there was just no holding him.

At that time Papa had twenty-five bird dogs, both setters and pointers. He preferred setters because their heavy coat protected them from the briars and bushes. I have seen our pointers with bloody tails where they had been cut by the briars as they thrashed through the rough and overgrown terrain.

Those were the days before radio and television and you were not bombarded at every turn by blatant ads for dog food. I can remember going into town on the streetcar and making the rounds of the kitchens of restaurants, picking up meat scraps for those darn dogs and I used to have to go out to the kennels at night, rain or shine, to feed them. It is a wonder that I still like dogs.

Mama kept after my father to get rid of some of his dogs and after he advertised in the sporting magazine we had a stream of visitors. One wealthy sportsman from Florida wanted a mature hunting dog which just fitted Jack's description and Papa, with some reluctance, decided to sell him. We took Jack and the sportsman into the fields and put on a performance. In the course of the afternoon we came to a split rail fence and just as Jack was climbing over he suddenly froze into a point. There was not a bit of cover anywhere around, nothing but bare ground and one small sassafras tree in the crotch of the fence.

Papa spoke gently to the dog. "Come on boy," he said but Jack wouldn't move. Then Papa tried boosting him over the fence but it was no good.

"Mr. Long, I think there's something the matter with that dog, why, there's no game around here," the man said.

About that time a cock pheasant flew right out of the top of that sassafras tree. (There are almost no pheasants in Tennessee, only an occasional stray bird, and old Jack was vindicated.) The man bought Jack on the spot.

Papa made a special trip back to the cabin where he had found Jack. The man wasn't home but Papa talked to his wife. "I bought a bird puppy from your husband several months ago and I wondered if you had any more of the litter."

"Wall no, we haint," the woman said. "His mother was a bird dog but the father was a big shepherd from up the creek. The one you got was the only one looked like a bird dog and the old man drowned the rest of 'em." Old Jack had inherited bird dog instinct from his mother and the strength and stamina of his big mountain shepherd sire!

There was one dog that Papa, for all his skill, couldn't handle. Somebody gave him a big heavyset bird dog called a "split-nose setter". I don't know if he was a special breed or just a freak of nature. His nostrils were separated so that you could lay your forefinger between them. We soon found out what prompted the generosity for he was the most vicious dog I have ever seen. He wouldn't let you touch him and Papa warned us to stay away from him. Papa used every trick he knew; even tried whipping him but that only served to make him worse. Finally he gave him to a farmer for a watchdog. I saw him later, chained to a tree and sounding his morose disagreement with everybody and everything around him.

One day Papa returned home from a fishing trip with a beautiful little pony hitched to a smart cart. He had bought it for my brother and me and driven all the way from Seiverville — twenty-five miles.

One of our prize setters was a female named Queen. Queen was allowed to run loose and she and the pony fell in love. It was wonderful to watch them playing in the pasture. When we came home after a ride Queen could hardly contain herself for joy. She would leap up and kiss Prince and she slept in his stall. She slept right under his feet and I have often seen him standing with one hind leg in the air to keep from stepping on her.

Papa, Mama, Frank and I often drove out into the country for a picnic and on this particular evening Queen lay to one side of the driveway and made no move to greet us. Papa took a sharp look at her and said, "That dog has been poisoned."

I haven't heard of a dog poisoner for some time but in those days . . . before riots, marches, and general hell-raising had come into fashion . . . certain sadistic goons worked off their hostility by poisoning dogs.

Queen couldn't move and Papa picked her up in his arms and laid her on the back porch. "Get me all the eggs you have and melt about a quart of lard," he told Mama. I held Queen's head and we forced two dozen eggs down her throat. she promptly vomited and when the eggs came up, they had turned bright green. "Strychnine," Papa said. The hot lard followed the eggs and that soon came up, too.

Papa sat up with Queen all night. Strychnine destroys the nervous system. "Everytime I took my hand off her head she would jump a foot," Papa told me. Fortunately we got to her in time and the eggs and lard had rid her stomach of enough of the poison so that she survived.

Papa's first dog was a big greyhound named Tony. Tony belonged to a traveling circus that was stranded in Leavenworth. His owner borrowed twenty-five dollars from grandfather and left the dog as security. He never returned to claim the animal. "I was fifteen and that dog was my pride and joy. My, how he could jump!" Papa said. "We had great sport chasing rabbits."

The greyhound is one of the few, perhaps the only dog

that hunts by sight. His nose is no good for smelling out game but he has keen eyes. Thus he was once called a "gazehound" and afterward his true name slipped over into "greyhound."

"I had great fun with that dog," Papa told me. "I would whisper 'Go lame, Tony' and he would run on three legs. 'Kip, your dog has gone lame,' my friends would say. 'Don't think so,' I'd say and when I snapped my fingers he would trot along on all four legs. He had a beautiful blanket with the name TONY emblazoned in letters that sparkled like diamonds."

Papa had a way with dogs. He spoke their language. "To get along with a dog you must first let him know that you respect him. Then it is only necessary to find a way to tell him what you expect of him. Given these circumstances he will go as far for you as his limited intelligence allows."

One late fall Papa and I were out quail shooting. We followed the dogs across a rail fence and into a pasture where we flushed a nice covey. Papa got two birds and I shot one. We were picking up our kill when an irate farmer emerged from woods at the top of the hill. He carried a pitchfork and was shouting, "Get off my land — no hunting allowed!" The covey had scattered and as he came storming into the pasture he kicked one of the birds out of the grass and it flew straight toward us. Papa calmly slung his gun to his shoulder and fired. It was a straight-on shot, a rather difficult target and he just winged the bird. Loosing aerial balance, it tumbled over and over but kept coming. Papa dropped his gun and as the quail came in at about eight feet, he leaped into the air and made a circus catch with one hand before the quarry hit the ground.

Well, the farmer saw the whole thing and by the time

Papa caught the bird he was standing stock still about a hundred yards away with his mouth open. Papa put the quail out of his misery and then walked up to the farmer. "I'm sorry we violated your land," he said. "We were not aware that we were on posted territory." "Mister," the farmer replied, "in all my born days I never see nothin' like it. I've seed many a bird shot on the wing but I never seed one caught afore it hit the ground. You can hunt on my farm any time you're a pleased to."

We stayed all night with that farmer and he and Papa sat up long after I had gone to bed "yarnin'" and partaking of refreshment.

CHAPTER 10

The Nativity on Tour

As I have told you, Papa was certainly no business man. He had the imagination but not the incentive for he had little or no desire to provide for a possible rainy day or to accumulate riches for the mere sake of accumulation. I suppose if Papa had been a Bible-quoting man one of his favorite verses would have been, "Take therefore no thought for the morrow: for the morrow shall take thought for the things of itself. Sufficient unto the day is the evil thereof." If Papa had faith, it was faith in himself and a total lack of fear of the unknown or of what life might hold for him at the next dawning. Sheer necessity, however, often drove him to devise ways to meet the needs of our family.

In Chapter Three I told you about Papa's "studio" on the banks of the Little River where he painted "The Nativity". It was a wonderful picture, heroic in size and I think one of the best things he ever did. The shepherds were clustered around the manger and there were sheep, goats and cattle in the foreground. These figures were in half shadow and a great light was focused on the Madonna and the infant Jesus. The central figures were of my mother and myself, taken from a painting he had done of us years before. Although I had no idea of his intentions it turned out that he was painting it for shadow-box display. He had a collapsible frame built, lined the sides with black cloth and directed a spotlight on the Child. When he displayed it he used wisps of straw and a water jug and an ancient looking cask in front of the picture. I tell you, the painting came alive and those who saw it stood silent and in awe.

The next summer Papa and I rolled up the huge canvas and hit the road. Papa mapped out our itinerary. We "played" small towns . . . those of about six thousand inhabitants were best . . . and we invited the local churches to sponsor the showing. I don't remember exactly how we divided the money from ticket sales but I know the church received the larger percentage. The price of admission was one dollar for adults, fifty cents for children, and the churches sold the tickets. After we had organized a town we rented a suitable place on the main street and opened for business. I took the tickets at the door and handled the finances.

When we started out Papa said, "Joe, we will be welcomed by the Baptists and the Methodists but the Presbyterians will not look with favor on us. The Presbyterians are cold fish." I afterward joined the Presbyterian church but I have no quarrel with Papa's appraisal of the Protestant denominations. It turned out exactly as he predicted.

We did very, very well and Papa got in some fishing, too.

I remember one place in the foothills of the Cumberland Mountains. We met one of the deacons of the Baptist

THE NATIVITY ON TOUR

church who proved to be an ardent disciple of Izaak Walton. Over the weekend he took us up to his camp in the mountains and we fished for three days. Our host was a regular fellow and he and Papa got on famously. He cast a good fly, swore appropriately when his fish got away and brought along an ample supply of warming drink for the end of the day.

Sitting around the fire one night Papa said, "Pete, how did you ever get to be deacon in the Baptist church? Somehow, you don't seem to fit the pattern."

"I'm not surprised you ask. I often wonder myself but a few of the larger contributors got together and decided that the rougher element needed representation and they picked me — I suppose it is a doubtful honor."

We were "on tour" for a little over a month and we cleared something over a thousand dollars but at the last stop we encountered a poor little church in the coal mine district that was struggling to survive. They had no piano so Papa gave away a good chunk of our profits so they might have one.

As I told you earlier, Papa was self-taught. He began his career as an artist at the age of ten when he drew a picture of his male teacher on the sidewalk in front of the school. It was far from flattering but unfortunately the likeness was unmistakable and he was made to pay dearly for his masterpiece.

He enjoyed portrait painting and because this branch of his art offered better earning possibilities, he did a great many portraits. He painted from sittings but he often had a number of photographs taken of his subjects and used these also. If a face didn't interest him, he refused to paint it no matter what the rewards.

Many of Papa's business dealings were clouded by financial misunderstandings. It seems that he had an aversion for having a firm agreement with his client about price. He had a hot temper and if his customer haggled with him he was apt to put the picture under his arm and walk off.

I am not absolutely sure that Papa was the hero of the following story but it fits his business pattern so completely that I shall make him the central character. He told it as follows: "An artist received a commission to paint a portrait of a small-town banker. He was the richest man in the county and lived in a handsome house on top of the hill overlooking his domain. The artist lived at the mansion and the banker sat for his picture over a period of two weeks. The price for the portrait was sort of left up in the air. When it was finished the banker and his family gathered for the unveiling. When the cloth was removed the wife and daughters, obviously afraid to express themselves until the great man had spoken, said nothing. 'What is your fee?' asked the banker.

" 'Two thousand dollars,' the artist replied.

"At this the banker flew into a rage. He declared that he would pay no such a ridiculous price. 'Why, the picture doesn't even look like me. No one would recognize it as my portrait.'

"The artist departed with the portrait and found lodgings in the town's hotel.

"Figuring that the banker's personality was ideally fitted for the making of enemies, he made discreet inquiries around town to find who the leader of this large group might be. Everywhere he received the same answer, 'Oh it's the Postmaster. They hate each other with a passion.'

"The artist visited the Post Office and explained his

dilemma to the Postmaster. I'm not at all surprised,' the Postmaster told him. 'That old blatherskite is hateful, underhanded, dishonest and any other reprehensible term that comes to mind. He has been bullying and cheating this community for years. I could have told you that he would never pay you a fair price for your work.'

" 'I would like to paint a couple of jackass ears on this picture and hang it in your Post Office,' the artist said.

" 'Well, it's against Postal regulations but this is too good a chance to miss. Go ahead and do it,' said the Postmaster.

"Next day just before the doors were thrown open the picture was hung. Two huge hairy ears sprouted from the bald head of the town's leading citizen. Of course the news spread like wildfire and all those able to walk came to see this wonderful picture. Here was an unexpected opportunity to ridicule the all-powerful. It seems there was hardly an individual within the city limits whose life had not in some way been blighted by the breath of this despot.

"In due course the attorney for the banker sought out the artist and threatened suit unless the portrait was immediately removed. 'The picture is libelous - you are defaming my client.'

" 'Not so,' the artist replied. 'He said the picture had no resemblance to him and I have three witnesses who heard him say it. I'll put them under oath and they will perjure themselves if they deny that he said it.'

"The lawyer apparently thought enough of this argument to consult with his client for he departed. After an hour he was back. 'My client will pay your fee if you will paint out the ears.'

" 'I'll be glad to but that will cost him another thousand,' the artist said. And so the matter was settled."

PAPA WAS A FISHERMAN

Papa painted the portraits of many famous people. At one time he received the commission to paint all the past governors of one of the western states. There were twenty-odd of them and most were painted from photographs, some of them old tintypes.

Papa used to tell a story about a struggling portrait painter who had something less to go on.

He was approached by a man who wanted a portrait of his father. "When can he sit for me?" the artist asked.

"Oh, he's been dead for twenty years," the prospect said. The artist, almost falling over himself in his eagerness for a commission, said that he often painted from photographs.

"As far as I know he never had a picture taken," the man told him.

Still reluctant to miss a much-needed fee the artist said, "You remember him, of course"

"Like yesterday," the man answered, "Why, I can see him right now."

"I can't guarantee the result but if you will describe him, the shape of his face, the color of his hair and eyes, I will be glad to see what I can do." And so it was arranged. Questioning the son closely the artist drew a sketch as best he could. At last came the time for the unveiling, but before showing the picture the artist enumerated his tremendous handicaps. "Oh, I understand all of that," the man said, "just show me Father."

The picture was unveiled and the son stood for some time examing it. "So that's Father, is it?" he asked.

"Well, its the very best I could do under the circumstances."

"The picture is fine and I'll take it," the man said, "but I was just thinking 'My God, how the old man has changed!' "

Papa was a great admirer of Lincoln and was given the commission to paint his portrait which hangs in the Lincoln Memorial at the Emancipator's birthplace in Hodgenville, Kentucky. The portrait is Papa's original conception of Lincoln. The figure is nine feet tall. He afterwards painted a smaller duplicate which hangs in the Lincoln National Bank in Louisville, Kentucky.

Papa loved animals and he painted many of them. As I write this I am sitting under a beautiful easel painting of Man-O-War. This is the picture which won him the commission to paint the official portrait of the great horse which is one and a half times life size and was hung in the Phoenix Hotel in Lexington. Following his painting of Man-O-War he lingered in Lexington and did many pictures of the thoroughbreds of the Blue Grass region.

Two outstanding attributes characterized Papa's art: his versatility, developed no doubt by the many things he was forced to do in order to support his family, and his genius for color. He ground many of his paints and the effects he produced were remarkable.

I have spoken of his independence. Some might say that he was too independent for his own good but, as I hope you now see, this made of him the rare individual that he was. In one of the towns where we put down our roots briefly there lived a wealthy man who owned the town's chief industry, a furniture-manufacturing plant. This man had come up from nothing and showed all the characteristics of newly acquired opulence. He called my father one day and asked him to come to his office.

"Mr. Long, I want you to paint my coat of arms on a new carriage I have bought," he offered.

"Not interested!" Papa said.

"And why not?"

"For two reasons . . . first, I am not a carriage painter and second, both of us know you don't have a coat of arms." Needless to say, this rebuff did not enhance Papa's chances in the community.

Papa had a friend who was a famous landscape painter. He was commissioned to paint the drop curtain for a new theater. The friend went to work but after a time he called Papa. "Long, I'm in trouble," he said. "Will you please come down to the theater and see what in God's name is the matter with my picture."

Papa came into the theater and stood studying the curtain from the back row. "Honestly, from that distance you couldn't tell what in the world the picture was about," he told me. "It was nothing but a mass of color.

"By the time I got to the front row I began to make out some detail but it still didn't hold together. I climbed the stairs to the stage and from ten feet away it was a beautiful landscape.

"The foliage had been done with a tiny brush, one similar to that used by my friend for his regular pictures. 'You are painting for the audience,' I told him. 'You paint the leaves of a tree with a sizing brush, not one of these.'

"Well, he asked me to illustrate and I did one corner of the curtain over while he sat in the back row. I ended up by doing the whole thing."

When Alf Landon ran for President his headquarters in one of the large cities commissiond Papa to do his portrait on a huge canvas which covered almost the entire front of a ten-story building. The head was forty feet in height. Papa had the canvas cut into six-foot squares and without a pattern he proceeded to paint the huge head in pieces. When they were sewed together there was the sunflower candidate bigger than life! That portrait could be called the only successful project of Landon's entire campaign!

CHAPTER 11

Special Delivery

In the Spring of 1932 Papa received a commission from a group of leading citizens of a large eastern city to paint the portrait of one of the foremost cancer research men in the world. The Doctor was hale and hearty in his seventies. In addition to his contributions to cancer research he had given a fortune to various projects in his city and his friends were trying to find a way to honor him. The portrait was to hang in the cancer clinic which had been largely built by his money.

It was decided that Papa was to live at the Doctor's home and paint from sittings. The two men got along famously. First off they both had the same attitudes toward money, and to bind the relationship the doctor was a fly fisherman.

Papa stayed with the Doctor for two months. During that time they snatched every chance to cast their flys upon the waters.

Papa had a way of studying his subjects which was somewhat disconcerting. I remember when he undertook my portrait. Often I would be aware that he was watching me. One day he came by the office. "Look me in the eyes," he ordered. I did so, and he shuddered. "You have a coldness in your eyes that disturbs me," he said. "Try to get a little more human kindness into them."

I am sure that those intimate times with the Doctor served him well for the portrait was not only the living image of his subject but there hung about it an aura of rare humanitarianism.

One afternoon Papa and the Doctor were sitting on the bank of a stream in the Poconos.

"Before you began my portrait I received the largest fee of my career," the Doctor told him. "I have a friend who is a multi-millionare. I've made repeated attempts to interest him in cancer research and various charities but I got nowhere. He is a strange self-made man who has some sort of aversion to sharing. I suppose it is not really his fault, probably stems from his early experiences. Well, at age forty-five he married for the first time, a lovely girl fifteen years younger and the daughter of one of my doctor friends. I had been very close to her father and had watched her grow into womanhood. Fact of the matter is I brought her into the world. As a young doctor I practiced obstetrics.

"One day my friend visited me at the Clinic and announced that they were going to have a baby and said he wanted me to deliver it. I refused. 'I haven't delivered a baby in many years,' I told him. 'Get some young man who has had up-to-date training. I simply won't risk it.'

"He was adamant. 'My wife and I will have nobody else-you simply must do it,' and then after a pause he said, 'you bring my child into the world, fill out a check for any amount and I'll sign it.'

"At this offer a diabolical scheme occured to me and I agreed.

"In due course the time arrived. The birth was a natural and an easy one but I had young obstetrician standing by in the wings, just in case.

"I've never seen two people happier with their first born. I waited a decent length of time and one morning I showed up at his office. 'I've come for my fee,' I told him. 'I could have sent you a bill but I wanted to present it in person.' He looked at me with the cold calculating stare which I am sure played no small part in his great financial success.

"I laid the check face down in front of him, the way they present the bad news to you in expensive restaurants. I wanted to see his face when he turned it over.

"He picked up one corner of the check as a man does when he is looking at a hole card in a poker game and then he flipped it face-up in front of him. It was for one hundred thousand dollars!

"He stared at it for some time and then a wry smile crept over his face. 'I remember our bargain,' he said, 'but Doc, you are putting a very strict limit on my progeny. Damned if I can afford many babies at that price.' Then he signed the check.

"I carried an envelope with me addressed to the Cancer Clinic and I picked up the check and sealed it inside. 'I've tricked you into doing what you should have done long ago,' I told him.

" 'You have just shared your good fortune with others and all because of that fine son of yours. Someday when he is

SPECIAL DELIVERY

old enough you will be proud to tell him about it and don't forget to take it off your income tax!'"

CHAPTER 12

"Fly Fishing is a Gentleman's Sport"

In the early 1900s before the game of golf had fastened its tentacles on those of the upper crust, before radio and television had captured the minds and consumed the idle hours of much of the population, before professional sports had turned us into a supine audience which gets its thrills vicariously, and before man himself had despoiled much of the wilderness by attempting to improve upon it . . . young and old turned to unadulterated nature for sport and recreation.

Papa's reputation as a fly fisherman spread far and wide and many came to him asking that he communicate the skills to themselves. Papa taught a great many men to fly fish and he also refused to teach a few. If Papa didn't like you, he wouldn't take you fishing. He could have made a great deal of money teaching fly casting; he could have opened a sporting goods store and made a great deal more for he was a sort of clearing house for the purchase of all sorts of gear. But

"FLY FISHING IS A GENTLEMAN'S SPORT"

Papa never thought of making money. He loved fishing and he was never too busy to help others enjoy it.

Some of Papa's pupils learned to catch fish with a fly and then some of them didn't. "Fishing is a gentleman's sport," Papa used to say, "and it also requires a certain temperament. I might say a good fly fisherman must have the proper philosophy not only about fishing but about life as well."

Papa told me about one of his pupils, a certain successful businessman, who was noted for his "killer instinct". He cast into a deep pool and hooked a bass. Immediately he threw the rod over his shoulder and started up the bank with his catch in tow. "Let him play! Let him play!" Papa yelled but the man kept going until he dragged the bass onto the bank. "Let him play! Hell," he shouted, "if he wants to play, let him play on the bank."

"That fellow will never make a fly fisherman," Papa said. "He just don't understand the sport."

This must have been the same fellow who was ordered by his doctor to get away from his business and out into the open. "You are driving hard toward a nervous breakdown and if you don't get your mind off your work and take regular exercise I can't be responsible for what happens," the doctor told him. "Now, what is it you like to do?"

"Nothing but work. I love to make money, that is my whole life."

"How about golf?" the physician asked.

This loosened a torrent of profanity about those who pursued a ball around a cow pasture and everything else the doctor mentioned was scorned by his patient. At last the man said, "Well, I think I would like to kill something - at least I would feel a sense of accomplishment." And so it was decided that he should try hunting.

He bought an expensive shotgun with a hand engraved barrel and set about advertising for the very best bird dog. He paid a big price for a champion Canadian setter and loaded down with the finest equipment, he and his dog set out for the hunt.

A month later the doctor encountered his patient on the street. "How is the hunting going?"

"Hell, I gave that up after two tries," the man said.

"What happened?" he was asked.

"Everything went wrong but it was mostly that damn dog. We'd get into a field and all of a sudden he would freeze and I couldn't get him to move. But I kicked him in the —— about twelve times and I want to tell you that I broke him of that."

It takes a long time to learn to catch fish consistently on a fly and many are never able to master the art. Papa told about one of his pupils who was fishing below him. "In the late afternoon I saw him a hundred yards ahead. He was sitting on a rock threshing about with something on the end of his line that I couldn't make out at that distance. As I got closer I saw that he had tied about twenty flies - all he had - on the end of his line. 'What in the world are you doing?' I asked him.

"'Well , Mr. Long,' he replied, 'I haven't had a single strike all day. I tried every one of these flies, too. Now I've got 'em all on my line, cafeteria style, and if they can't find something interesting in this bunch I've got nothing else to offer and I'm going home!'"

It was pretty discouraging to watch Papa fish. We were out with a couple of Papa's friends one day. The three of us weren't having any luck and we seated ourselves on the bank to watch the professional. He cast behind a rock and his rod

"FLY FISHING IS A GENTLEMAN'S SPORT"

bent as the fish struck. Papa began reeling in when suddenly the rod was almost torn from his grasp. His catch leaped into the air and lo-and-behold there were not one but two fish on his line, a big bass and a small "red-eye" or rock bass glued together. The next time they broke water the two fish were ten yards apart. After quite a battle Papa landed the fish and explained the phenomenon to his goggle-eyed audience. The large-mouth bass has a mouth as big as his entire girth. He wasn't hooked at all but the line was run through one of his gills and he couldn't get free because of the red eye on the hook. "The red eye struck and the bass went after the red eye, his big mouth wide open. In his attempt to escape, the red eye ran right through the gills of the bass and he was strung up hard and fast."

This episode added to Papa's fame as the man who could catch two fish on one fly!

Papa belonged to a fishing and hunting club in the Cumberland Mountains. The Emery River ran through the property and in the deep holes of this stream lurked the savage muskellunge. If the clubhouse is still standing you will find on the oak front door the outline of a "muskie" which Papa caught and traced there. It was the largest ever taken from the Emery.

The muskie is a formidable looking fish. He has a torpedo shaped body and an ugly mouth in which are set two rows of evil looking teeth. He is a mean rascal and will attack a lure whether he is hungry or not.

We made a trip to the Cumberlands and took along one of Papa's friends who wanted to learn to fish. We floated down the Emery in a rowboat and Papa was showing his friend how to cast a plug. Suddenly from behind a sunken log a big muskie made for the lure. The water was clear and we could see the huge shape, mouth open, boiling up after the artificial minnow. The caster saw it, too, and he began to reel in and jerk the lure away from the fish. The muskie kept coming. "Let him have it! Let him have it!" Papa yelled, but his pupil paid no attention.

"He's not going to get this," the man shouted and he finally jerked the minnow clear out of the water and away from the fish who had followed it right up to the boat. Then it dawned on him what he had done and chagrin set in. We all had a good laugh.

"Just one thing," our companion said, "please, Mr. Long, don't ever tell this. If you do I'll have to move out of town."

Most of Papa's fly fishing pupils belonged to what today would be the golfing set but there was one exception. He was a man whom I shall call John Penner. He was a pawnbroker and his story is an interesting one.

Penner was no more than five feet five. He was stooped, totally bald, and he had an eye that pierced you like a knife. I remember that he always wore a stiff white shirt, a white laundered narrow bow tie and in the center of the hard front of his shirt there glittered a huge diamond. He was certainly what the East Tennesseeans referred to as a "furriner" but I never learned his place of origin. He had come to Knoxville years before with a pushcart from which he sold cheap jewelry. One day he saw a man drop a package on the street. Penner retrieved it and found that it contained a bank deposit of several hundred dollars. He kept the money, used it to open a pawn shop, and some years later sent it all back anonymously plus six percent interest.

I don't know how he and Papa got acquainted, perhaps during one of his "no money" periods Papa placed the family jewels in hock. Penner was very fond of Papa and he often

"FLY FISHING IS A GENTLEMAN'S SPORT"

came to our home. One night he told how he had bought several violins and antiqued them. They had brought back his investment a hundredfold, he said.

"Why Mr. Penner," my mother remonstrated, "I'm surprised at you . . . that is downright dishonest." This seemed a totally new idea to Penner and it left him speechless.

Penner made a fortune out of his business. He lived in a mansion and owned three big automobiles, none of which he ever learned to drive. He decided to sell his business and enjoy himself.

The purchasers of his business came down from the East to take stock. They were a couple of smart Jewish gentlemen.

Penner sat in the store while they were checking his merchandise and he was much disturbed when they began to talk to each other in Yiddish. Max Finklestein had a cut-rate clothing store next door and Penner approached Finklestein one morning. "Max, do you take a Yiddish newspaper?" he asked.

"Sure do," Max said. "Here is yesterday's paper." Penner had Max interpret a few of the headlines for him and then he carried it back to the pawnshop. He sat down and began to study it. When he was sure the two men were watching he began to read aloud. "I see that," and he annouced a few of the headlines. "Those fellers never talked Yiddish again," he told Papa.

Penner asked Papa to teach him to fly fish. Papa took him up into the Smokies to one of his favorite haunts. They caught many fish. They ate supper and spent the night in a mountain cabin, occupying the only bedroom. When they were ready to leave Papa offered to pay for their lodging. "We don't want no money," the woman said. "You'nses is welcome to what we have." Papa insisted and at last under his urging the woman said, "Well, I guess a dollar apiece."

"How about fifty cents?" Penner suggested. Papa silenced him with an icy stare and thrust five dollars into her hand.

When they were outside Papa said, "John, this is the last time I'll ever take you fishing."

"Why?" Penner asked. "I like it. I'm having a wonderful time."

"I'll never take you again," Papa repeated, "because fly fishing is a gentleman's sport and you're no gentleman!"

In the days before the National Park was established there were only a few mountain hotels One of these was situated on Little River facing a deep pool. Papa and I were staying the night and just at dark, working his way downstream, Papa hung a big bass right in front of the hotel. The fish maneuvered under a sunken log and fouled the line. Papa tried unsuccessfully to free it and finally cut the line and came to dinner.

The next morning just at dawn he put on his bathrobe, slipped through the deserted lobby and made his way down the path to the stream. He plunged naked into the icy water, dived down ten feet and began to grope under the log. A couple of times he had to come up for air but on the third try he located the bass, still fast to the broken line which was caught around the snag. He got his fingers into the gills and jerked him loose. Coming to the surface with his fish he spied three young ladies standing beside his robe and grinning at Papa's imagined embarrassment. Taking in the situation at a glance, Papa calmly climbed onto the bank, bade them a cheery Good Morning and making no attempt to hold the big bass in an advantageous position he walked toward his spectators.

"FLY FISHING IS A GENTLEMAN'S SPORT"

For a moment the young ladies stood rooted to the spot, their mouths open. Then they fled in utter rout.

This is somehow reminiscent - Papa, the indominable Fisherman, rising like Triton from the deep, facing the world naked and unafraid!

Now the wilderness and Papa have departed and I am glad that they have gone together for I am sure if he could come back to visit the old haunts that the change would sadden him. Macadam roads have replaced the old trails. Motels and knick-knack shops clutter the mountain towns. Tame bears roam the roads begging for food from tourists who litter this ancient land with their refuse.

Uniformed Rangers are everywhere, picking up paper plates and keeping everybody in line. The tourists manage to get out of their cars at various look-out points to complain about the mist from which these majestic peaks have earned their name. Disappointed, they return to the Motel and the martini, which turns out to be the highlight of the day.

A few venture onto the trails and if you walk far enough, solitude of a sort can be found but one cannot escape the knowledge that civilization is but a short distance away.

The Mountaineer is uprooted and scattered to the low lands and his children have been seduced by the mores of the times. The mountain songs are sung against the backdrop of folk festival platforms and they have lost much of their plaintiveness.

At some far-distant time the wilderness will perhaps return, for the ways of Nature are everlasting. If that day comes the feeble scratchings of Man upon the surface of the hills will be obliterated. The dams will crumble and the streams return to their old channels.

I can imagine that some distant relative of yours and mine

will find his way back into this solitude and that in his simplicity he will lift up his eyes unto the hills from whence cometh his help and that his mind will grasp what his sophisticated Ancestor became too blind to see.

If there is to be a new beginning then Adam must be born again.

I think a man like Papa would make a very fine Adam!